The Afterlife of Gardens

PENN STUDIES IN LANDSCAPE ARCHITECTURE
John Dixon Hunt
Series Editor

This series is dedicated to the study and promotion of a wide variety of approaches to landscape architecture, with special emphasis on connections between theory and practice. It includes monographs on key topics in history and theory, descriptions of projects by both established and rising designers, translations of major foreign-language texts, anthologies of theoretical and historical writings on classic issues, and critical writing by members of the profession of landscape architecture.

The Afterlife of Gardens

John Dixon Hunt

UNIVERSITY OF PENNSYLVANIA PRESS

Philadelphia

For Andrew and Matthew, with love

Originally published 2004 by REAKTION BOOKS LTD
79 Farringdon Road
London EC1M 3JU, UK

www.reaktionbooks.co.uk

First published in the United States 2004 by
University of Pennsylvania Press
Philadelphia, Pennsylvania 19104-4011

Cataloguing-in-Publication data is available from the Library of Congress

ISBN 0-8122-3846-X

Contents

Preface

This is a book about how gardens and other kinds of designed landscape have been experienced or received. It argues for the reception or 'afterlife' of sites rather than the processes of their design and implementation. The study of gardens has largely treated them as a series of design initiatives; historiographically, that has meant isolating and narrating the high points of stylistic changes, mainly focusing on leading examples of design in each period and culture. A reception study will not displace that well-established approach, but it does offer exciting and fresh perspectives on garden culture by exploring how sites are experienced, often through a *longue durée* of existence, change and reformulation.

The opening essay argues the case for a reception study of gardens, asking how the procedures of reception theory long established in literary studies might be adapted for use in the discussion of designed landscapes. Next comes a segment on the garden as 'virtual reality', which looks at ways in which sites trigger the imaginations of their visitors. Then, to counter the general impression that the experience of gardens became a vital consideration in theory and practice only at the time of the Picturesque garden in the later eighteenth century, some early examples are explored: first, the early illustrated book, the *Hypnerotomachia Poliphili*, published in Venice in 1499, is read as an early example of a deliberate and sustained interest in how its protagonist experiences the gardens and landscapes through which his love quest takes him. Moving from fictional to real gardens, the next three essays take up the themes of how the design of gardens can stimulate visitors' imaginations through the invention of architectural items (*fabriques*) and inscriptions; how different modes of response – words and different genres of writing, or graphic imagery of different sorts – were invoked to articulate responses to those and other elements of the landscape; and how movement makes a fundamental contribution to the process of garden reception. The detailed discussions of this collection are concluded with a look at the somewhat different receptions of landscape that modern motorists experience, both at high speeds and at those moments of rest that lengthy and fast road travel requires of them.

During these segments various sites are invoked as illustrations of the more general discussions, and it is hoped that the reader will understand that the recurrence of these examples – notably Versailles, Méréville, Moulin Joli, Stowe and Central Park, among others – as different themes are addressed will suggest the rewards of re-examining sites that are generally well researched and well understood in the usual historical narratives but which can be seen afresh in the light of reception theory. It is also worth pointing out here that the term *garden* is used both in a conventional sense – to indicate a finite space formally marked off and designed with often a concentration of effects – and further to imply the *idea* of the garden that infects the design work of landscape architecture on sites and across scales for which the term garden does not seem apt. (I have argued the case for this *idea* of the garden in *Greater Perfections*, 2001.)

A final essay returns to some of the propositions of the first and sets out at more length my claims for a reception study of gardens and its importance in both historical study and contemporary practice. Here the idea of an Implied Visitor is borrowed from literary reception theory (its Implied Reader) and adapted in the light of the various sites that have been the key case studies throughout the book. The usefulness of the Implied Visitor for approaches to historical preservation is also proposed.

The first and last essays of *The Afterlife of Gardens* are newly composed for this collection. The others are revised versions, in most cases substantially reworked, of lectures delivered or pieces previously published. Though those occasionally or indirectly touched on matters of reception, I have been able to reformulate their arguments and introduce new examples in the light of a topic that has become the focus of my current teaching and research. I am grateful, nonetheless, to those publications where articles originally appeared: that on the *Hypnerotomachia* was published in *Word & Image*, XIV (1998); that on the garden as virtual reality in a special issue of *Die Gartenkunst* (1997), *Das Künstliche Paradies: Gartenkunst im Spammungsfeld von Natur und Gesellschaft*, edited by Marcus Kohler; those on movement were drawn both from a paper delivered at a Dumbarton Oaks symposium and subsequently published in *Landscape Design and the Experience of Motion*, edited by Michel Conan (2003), and from an essay, 'Arrêts de hazard sur l'autoroute', in *Autoroutes et paysages*, edited by Christian Leyrit and Bernard Lassus (Paris, 1994). Other essays have grown out of lectures delivered at Bristol University (the Perry Art Lecture in 2003), St John's College, Oxford (the Robert Penson lecture, 2002), Skidmore College (the 2001 Adler Lecture), the Fundação Serralves in Portugal, a garden conference organized by the Bundesdenkmalamt in Vienna in 2002, and a Word and Image Conference in Paris in 2003 organized jointly by the University of Paris VII and Holy Cross College, and to those various audiences and their reactions I am grateful. I am also grateful to colleagues who have read and advised on and otherwise contributed to drafts of these essays: Anita Berrizbeitia, Emily Cooperman, David Leatherbarrow, Frank Matero and Laurie Olin. A special word of thanks, also, to Tricia Rubenstein, my research assistant in the final stages of making this book.

ONE

A Reception History of Landscape Architecture

I

This book is about how gardens can be experienced, not about
how they have been designed. It must be admitted, however,
that narratives and criticism about the design of gardens are the
more usual, for many reasons. We are readily drawn to a study
of origins, especially if those stories concern famous designers
or patrons; also, historians tend to write about a sequence of
cutting-edge events or (in art) new, formal developments.
Generally speaking, too, the documentation for gardens, if it
survives at all, is focused on the initiation of sites (or major
revisions or renewals of those sites), while the material for
subsequent visits to and experiences of them seems less available.[1]
And when we are concerned with contemporary landscape
architecture, both journalistic and academic approaches privilege
creators and designers, who are often themselves the exponents
of their own work,[2] and, of course, in recent examples there is
anyway not yet sufficient evidence of the uses and reception
of a site to sustain an alternative enquiry.

Yet it must be acknowledged that how gardens are visited,
how they are used (and perhaps abused), and how they are
absorbed into the experiences of generations of people who
explore them after their creation constitute a very different and
just as fascinating a story. Especially when a site has been in
existence for some time, attitudes to it will respond to the
changes that have occurred within it (in what is after all one of

the more fragile of art forms), including alterations in ownership and access, and will also reflect fresh ideas and assumptions of the men and women who are still drawn into its orbit. Even a site particularly famous at its inception, hailed perhaps for its pioneering scenes and materials, will survive in changed forms and exist for changed times.

Soon after the death of the Irish poet W. B. Yeats in 1939, and in celebration of his continuing literary existence, W. H. Auden wrote that the 'words of a dead man are modified in the guts of the living' ('In Memory of W. B. Yeats'). He meant, of course, that a poet, especially a dead one, cannot control how we read and understand his poetry, but that – especially if it is good – we will constantly re-read it in new ways; so even when later generations repeat the very same words that Yeats originally published, they will probably give them new meanings and new resonance. When we are dealing with materials in a garden that have neither denotative basis (as words do in the first instance) nor precise declarations of idea or emotion, there is considerably more scope for re-investing them with fresh meanings, for seeing them in different ways than were ever originally intended or anticipated. That, then, is the subject of this collection of essays – to study how gardens may be experienced and to explore the *longue durée* of reception rather than the often more brief moment of design or inception.

II

Gardenists (I use this coinage of Horace Walpole because it embraces both those who make and those who study gardens) might usefully be reminded that reception has been studied in other arts. Indeed, there is a considerable body of writing on reception theory as it relates to literature, to which any radical change that might be contemplated in garden historiography might profitably apply itself. However, the literature on reception theory is extensive and not at all homogenous;[3] nor, most obviously, does a method developed for written texts transfer automatically or easily to landscape architecture. Yet it would be impossible to take up the role of visitors' responses to or receptions of gardens without proposing some structure by which such an analysis could be conducted beyond the merely anecdotal and empirical, and since the makings of such a conceptual framework lie to hand in literary reception theory, it is convenient to adapt elements of that for our own purposes.

I rehearse here a series of positions and moves in reception theory that could probably be useful for the work of a gardenist, and in each case I have tried to consider what adjustments (minor or radical) would be required for their application in garden and landscape studies. A fundamental difference that grounds the qualifications that follow was voiced by one of the reception theorists himself, though not of course with any reference to landscape architecture. Wolfgang Iser distinguished between the real world that is accessible to the senses and exists outside any description of it and a literary work that is 'only accessible' to the imagination.[4] We might modify this claim by remarking how a garden partakes of both conditions, thereby providing a more interesting, a richer and even more ambiguous object of reception study.

There are basically two modes of reception theory: the German word *Rezeption* points to readers' judgement of a text, while *Wirkung* directs attention to the potential effect of the text, to the interaction with its readers. We shall need to extend this distinction to one that separates, on the one hand, responses to a garden that seek to understand, judge or explain it from those that seek to articulate a visitor's interaction with it; even so, the distinction can be hard to make in practice.

Rezeption particularly is concerned with a reader's grasp of meaning in a literary text. But, as Jane Tomkins notes, this is a very modern concern, since from Classical times to at least the mid-eighteenth century meaning was taken for granted, and what was discussed instead were both the means by which such and such a meaning was communicated and, given that rhetorical manipulation, the morality or public responsibilities of such persuasion. Texts were instruments of social thought and policy, and this emphasis on social relevance simply allowed the meaning of the text, the text as an object of scrutiny in its own right, to be assumed. Once that social aspect of writing ceased to be central, the focus switched effectively to the text's meaning, the assimilation of which reception theory strives to understand. In gardenist matters, we shall therefore need, first, to attend to the historical moment of meaning in garden experience, since it is not entirely clear that such responses paralleled those for literature; it seems clear, for instance, that the early Renaissance garden elicited as much attention to what it could 'say' to visitors as to any 'rhetorical' and political obligations or expectations. But, secondarily, it is also clear that to understand what 'meanings' we should expect of landscape architecture is equally important for garden studies.

The modern, formalist aspect of reception theory encounters two famous 'fallacies', both advanced and discussed by W. K. Wimsatt and Monroe C. Beardsley:[5] the Intentional Fallacy required us to avoid using implied or even actual authorial explanations of intent in literary analysis, and the Affective Fallacy repudiated confusions between the text and its results or psychological effects. The Intentional Fallacy is countered in reception theory by involving the reader in determining meanings, thus avoiding the contentious issues of whether interpretative authority lies with the author and of what can be read in a text as opposed to read into it; this is partly the issue that W. H. Auden addresses when he argues that Yeats's poetry will enjoy a life of its own after the poet's death. The Affective Fallacy, on the contrary, is welcomed by reception theory, for the reason that there can be no effective meaning outside its realization in the mind of a reader. These literary debates focus on meaning, which, as has already been suggested, proves to be a rather thorny problem in landscape architecture.

Some reception theory also mediates the relationship between past and present, rather than merely accepting received tradition. The usefulness of this perspective for garden studies is obvious, since the traditional, historical or original reading of a garden pertains to a site that inevitably will have changed; the very process of its evolution into the present day demands new responses that have to be accommodated in some fashion with earlier ones.

The closeness of some literary reception studies to a phenomenology of reading ensures a deliberate convergence or merging of subject and object, particularly in the work of the French critic Georges Poulet, who achieves what Elizabeth Freund calls an 'astonishing intimacy' between the two.[6] Much garden writing falls unthinkingly into this collusion between consciousness and the objects that prompt it, a collusion where externality or the garden's physical forms seem to lose ground to interiority, to the sometimes sentimental meditations on the idea of a garden.[7] This can indeed be a most un-strenuous activity and is usually dismissed as negligible by critics and historians. Yet at its best it can be a remarkable resource, if we are trying to understand how the phenomenal, material world of gardens is received in the minds and imaginations of those who encounter it.

As such a resource, the phenomenology of landscape enjoys a stronger hold on the object than seems the case in much literary readings. For there is, irrefutably in the study of gardens, though endlessly debated and problematic in literary criticism, both an object with 'brute-fact' status and the concretization or realization of that object by visitors who smell, touch, see or otherwise feel it and then graphically or verbally represent their experience of a distinct, physical site. This double obligation to both the actuality or reality of a site and to the visitor's own subjectivity should prevent merely solipsist or wholly 'virtual' responses to a garden on the one hand and a merely descriptive, even positivist attempt to record its elements on the other.

The interaction between a literary text and the reader's processing of it takes place in certain conditions that control that interaction; these have to do with genre, tone, structure, etc., as well as the social conditions in which it is read. The same is true of a garden, except that conventions and circumstances are different, even unique to that art; it uses different materials, involves the spatial experience of perambulation and (prime among the senses) viewing, and draws on assumptions that visitors bring with them about garden art and its different 'genres', such as public square, cemetery, sculpture garden and so on. A garden has its own repertoire of natural effects and artificial insertions that exist independently of a visitor's acts of comprehension, even though they may be the means by which some signals are exchanged between them. Like a text, although via its own unique formulations, a garden may propose or even instruct, and its visitors dispose or construct meanings and experiences from that; it is what Wolfgang Iser has termed a dynamic happening,[8] for without stimuli or triggers, no response or interpretation will be forthcoming. But while the literary text has neither a chance to talk back, correct or supplement the reader's responses nor an objective status by which wholly to dictate readings, a garden, while not exactly talking back, is palpably, haptically there – with the result that, independent of its visitors' reactions, its physical presence can directly challenge their reactions and responses to it.[9]

Iser has famously proposed the concept of an Implied Reader, who is a construct and not to be identified with any real reader; even though that Implied Reader has presumably to be put together in part from evidence collected from actual readings. It may be useful for the garden historian also to explore the idea of an Implied Visitor, constituted in the same fashion from a concatenation of actual responses in real time and space. Given such an Implied Visitor, the garden will be constructed 'only as a series of changing viewpoints, each one restricted in itself' (this is Iser, invoking the metaphor of a journey, a useful analogy for garden visits).[10]

It follows, finally, that no single experience of a garden, as no one reading of a literary text, can exhaust its full potential. That potential, indeed, is surely one of the prime characteristics of great landscape creations (and we are or must be also concerned with quality, with identifying the best examples of this art). This potency presents itself as an otherness, or rather a fullness, outside and beyond our personal, local or any other particular experience of the site; it is that potential in a site, of course, that calls for repeated visits. As historians, we have a double opportunity to recover this potential in an existing site: one is by our own actual and repeated visits and responses; the other is by accumulating the reports of others who have been there at other times and in other circumstances that we may not even imagine until we listen to and view them attentively. This last mode is our only resource when a physical site has disappeared.

III

The history of landscape architecture is narrated almost exclusively from the point of view of the original designs and their designers. Where sites are modified in subsequent cultural episodes, these changes, too, are described in terms of design intention. Yet if gardens survive – Versailles, the Villa d'Este, Stowe, Central Park – their survival is due as much to their reception, to how they can be the object of renewed and renewing responses through different generations and cultural changes subsequent to the moment of their creation. Where they have not physically survived – Moulin Joli, Yuanming Yuan, the original Pratolino of the Medici, Pliny's Tuscan villa or Horace's Sabine farm – we are (if lucky) dependent either on original archives and / or archaeological remains that document the original design, or on the records of visitors who knew the sites before their destruction or disappearance. Certainly, no history of gardens is likely to ignore their reception by different visitors; yet their testimony is invoked most usually to substantiate what we know from other sources of the original design process or even – implicitly and by sleight of hand – to take the place of such sources that are no longer available. In fact, no history of gardens has been constructed from the privileged point of view of those who experienced rather than designed them. It would for one thing be a huge undertaking, simply because, if it is specific responses to a garden that we are interested in, we shall need to assemble considerable quantities of them before we can establish any general pattern, of the sort that has been, for better or for worse, laid down for a narrative of design history. It may well be, in that case, that the resources of a reception history will be expended on specific sites.

Yet we need to ask at this stage what exactly a narrative of gardens, based on such assumptions and procedures, would look like. It is unlikely, for instance, that key sites would cease to have importance – Stowe, Versailles, Wörlitz, and so on. But their designers would play a far less significant role unless their involvement was absorbed as part of the mythology of reception – that is, the almost pious reverence for Le Nôtre or 'Capability' Brown caught up in a visitor's response to a garden either designed by him or thought to be so. However, gardens without the kudos of named architects behind them are far more likely to be brought into the discussion once we obtain records of their visitation; this would pull in much urban, vernacular and even imaginary garden-making (in novels, paintings, poems).

The conditions of a response will clearly affect it: in other words, we should ask of historical site descriptions as of modern analyses of newly built work whether the respondents are speaking from direct experience of the site or from a priori knowledge of different sorts (has the visitor read a guidebook, for instance, or is affected by the particular acclaim of a site?); the motives and assumptions of visitors assume a major importance here. Distinctions would also need to be made between visitations by outsiders and those by owners, family members or close associates, and these latter in their turn would necessarily draw upon what could be determined of the latter's insider knowledge of the original design process.

Stylistic patterns and art-historical labels – especially terms such as 'formal' and 'informal', 'Rococo' and 'Baroque', an inert terminology so appealing to historians – would cease to be privileged unless visitors could be shown to have responded in those very terms themselves. An intriguing example here is the invocation by European garden visitors in the late eighteenth century of 'pictures' in the landscapes visited: we need to try and recover more nuanced ideas of what their assumptions were about the phenomenon that we, too, generically label 'the Picturesque'. When, for instance, the Italian Francesco Bettini visited Blenheim in 1777 and exclaimed that 'at every step I encountered pleasing pictures',[11] it would be useful to know whether he was simply acknowledging the fact of a designed scenery (as a painter 'designs' or lays out his canvas), whether he actually associated existing pictorial imagery with the Oxfordshire site, or whether, as he roamed, he was inventing pictures either in the landscape or in his imagination.

The new history would obviously depend on verbal and visual representations of sites after the fact of their creation, and particularly precious here would be sketches, maps or other records in which visitors obviously tried to encode their impressions; we also have imagery (and indeed verbal reports) that were in some sense commissioned to represent a required or official point of view – Louis XIV's Versailles produced any number of these, but arguably so did early English landscape gardens such as Chiswick and Stowe.[12] Both of these kinds of evidence would need to be distinguished from the body of materials that grew out of the design process itself.

Two examples – one Western (Méréville), the other Eastern (Yuanming Yuan) – will illustrate both the complexities and the potential excitements of exploring the various representations of a site. Neither site exists in anything like its original splendour; for the very ruined Chinese site, less so for the French, we are therefore dependent on the records of many visitations.[13] Méréville (illus. 1) is now denuded of its many wonderful *fabriques*,

1 One of the rock bridges at Méréville today.

2 Hubert Robert, *Méréville: The Rustic Bridge and the Temple of Filial Piety. c.* 1790, oil on canvas.

which were removed in the 1920s to another park at Jeurre, where they survive; the vegetation has of course changed considerably since the late eighteenth century, when the Marquis de Laborde commissioned the design in the years before the Revolution; and the château itself is now unoccupied, with direct consequences for the use and upkeep of the park. But we have a series of remarkable paintings by Hubert Robert (illus. 2), who was responsible for much of the original creation: yet it is impossible to know whether these are projections, that is to say design proposals, or whether they record built work along with examples of its inhabitation, or even whether they are examples of a designer projecting not only a design but elements of its potential reception as well. Furthermore, what happens when a series of largely photographic images of Méréville much later in its existence (illus. 3) intervene in our understanding of its original layout? Do we simply discount these impressions as irrelevant, to be

erased in mental and even perhaps in physical reconstructions?
Yet the physical site – a striking valley, surrounded by low ridges,
with a meandering stream through it – is not the same today as is
shown in Robert's paintings, nor of course do we probably look
at scenery in anything like the same way as he did. So altogether
we can never recover the original experience of Méréville, even if
we were to enhance photographs of the present landscape digitally
with the missing temples and other removed items.

Even more is this the case with Yuanming Yuan, a complex
eighteenth-century garden or series of gardens that has now
almost wholly disappeared and cannot be 'seen' other than
through the conceptions of those who knew it, as did the Jesuit
father Jean Denis Attiret (1702–68), who was there during the
final period of its construction in the early eighteenth century.

Even though he said the 'only way to conceive it is to see it', what we are able to 'see' are the visual and verbal records by those who experienced this exceptionally intricate site. These are themselves problematic, for we have different Western and Chinese perspectives, but also Western imagery created for Chinese consumption and vice versa; we also have paintings commissioned to celebrate the establishment of different gardens in the overall complex of Yuanming Yuan, but like Western counterparts – one thinks of Hubert Robert's paintings of Méréville – these may blur the representation of built work and the projection of its design (illus. 4 and 5). Further, we have visual and verbal responses to the site in the years after its creation, more after its destruction by Anglo-French forces in 1860, some

4 The Yuanming Yuan, from the anonymous series *40 Scenes of the Garden of Perfect Clarity*, *c.* 1744, ink and wash on paper.

5 A marble bridge in a part of the Yuanming Yuan known as Jingming Yuan, in 1912.

subsequent attempts at restoration later in the nineteenth century, its abuse during the Cultural Revolution and its rehabilitation more recently: all these moments and locations in its history make up a complex history of reception. Indeed, since Yuanming, like Méréville in part, no longer exists in anything except the responses of many, many observant visitors, we bring ourselves close to having to accept that it exists now only in its palimpsestial reception. Although its existence in that form is more complex or complicated, it is also more enduring, and reception even becomes the only true form of historic preservation.

IV

As the case of Yuanming Yuan suggests, there can be abundant material for a reception history of many gardens, especially if it is handled in a way to yield its distinctive perspectives, some of which will inevitably provide valuable insights for designers who wish to anticipate the afterlife of their creations. However, it is also clear that certain sites and certain kinds of garden have elicited a more prolific repertoire of responses than others for which the design history is more crucial and so attracts more attention. The most obvious cases are those gardens that have never existed, or if they did, now survive in myth and legend: Eden, for instance, or the Hanging Gardens of Babylon, or such an imaginary Chinese garden as that described in the sixteenth century by Liu Shilong.[14] But a further case of gardens with a high reception potential are those that came into being during the later eighteenth century, sometimes called 'Picturesque', 'natural' or even 'modern' gardens, and which seem to have elicited a spate of responses, distinct from directions about their design, that far exceeds similar material from earlier or later gardens.[15]

The Garden of Eden, a prototypical, if unique, case of a site lost to subsequent visitors, exists entirely and solely in the words and images of those who were there originally (its designer, God, and Adam and Eve, as reported in the biblical book of Genesis); other accounts come from those who have been forced to visit it in their imaginations (illus. 6), which is pure reception, unfettered

6 'The Expulsion from Eden' in an anonymous late 15th-century Flemish woodcut.

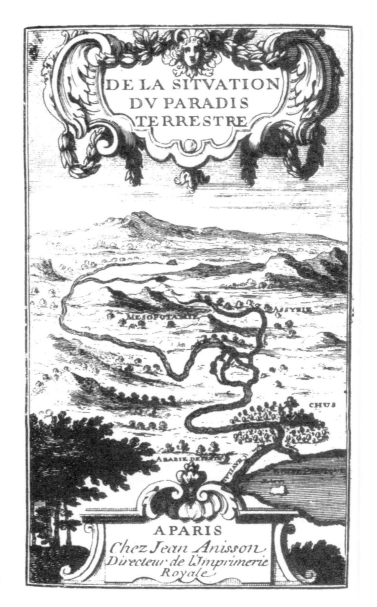

DE LA SITVATION
DV PARADIS
TERRESTRE

MESOPOTAMIE

ASSYRIE

CHUS

ARABIE DESERTE

A PARIS
Chez Jean Anisson
Directeur de l'Imprimerie
Royale

7 Title-page of
Pierre-Daniel Huet,
*Traité de la Situation du
Paradis Terrestre* (Paris,
1691).

by circumstantial evidence; even medieval and Renaissance attempts to map its location (illus. 7) were largely unconstrained by geographical realities. Inasmuch as garden history always seems to depart from this original and prototypical site, it is odd that more analysis has not focused on reception rather than design. For of the design of Eden, Genesis tells us simply three things: that the garden was 'eastward' and 'in Eden'; that it was watered by a river that had its source in Eden, after which the river was divided into 'four heads' that flowed to different points of the compass; and, third, that it contained all natural history ('every tree that is pleasant to the sight, and good for food', and 'Every beast of the field, and every fowl of the air'). As a design report or programme, this is not very precise, and it has accordingly afforded scope for the imagination of those who were never there; that, of course, means all but two garden visitors, and even those are reported at second-hand! The design of Eden has in most cases been read as a reflection of the culture that wished to revisit and 'preserve' it. Horace Walpole joked that the French thought Eden must have been like Versailles; seventeenth-century Flemish painters transformed it into a rich panorama of natural curiosities that paralleled the *kunst- und wunderkammern* in vogue at that time (illus. 8); the German garden theorist Hirschfeld refused to speculate — as he felt every previous garden history had done — on whether Eden was like a French or an English garden precisely, one suspects, because his own theory of garden art envisaged an inclusive reliance on neither of those styles. Everybody could make Eden in his or her own image, simply because the original was not there to confront and confound their particular theory; Eden exists, in short, in and via its reception.[16]

What we might term the 'Eden effect' (or the 'idea' of Eden) is widespread in the reception of even those gardens that do survive in some form and for which we have empirical evidence of their existence. This 'Eden effect' tries to bring the actual,

8 Peter Paul Rubens and Jan Brueghel II, *Adam and Eve in the Garden of Eden*, *c.* 1630, oil on canvas.

historical site closer to the primordial model (however a given culture chooses to construct that model). In this strategy the reception of all gardens and landscapes tends to the Edenic and to contain a paradisal strain, an acknowledgement of the *ur*-garden, the garden to end (and begin) all gardens. While some will condemn this as wayward fantasy, a mere 'sentimental aestheticization',[17] its pervasive influence on garden reception (as on garden design) cannot be dismissed, and it is part of a whole repertoire of garden assumptions that we see more clearly expressed in imaginary writings, film and paintings about gardens,[18] which are perhaps a culture's most persistent efforts to 'receive' Eden.

But there are other cultural assumptions about gardens that affect reception of them. Where this is most insistent is precisely when an interest in garden experience and reception begins to prevail over an interest in design principles – namely, with writings on the Picturesque or what Horace Walpole called the 'modern' garden. It was Georg Gadamer who insisted upon the modernity of 'experience',[19] and we should therefore not be surprised that an increased absorption in how gardens were experienced enters into accounts of what is arguably the watershed of modernity in landscape architecture as in other areas. As later essays will explore in more detail, the Picturesque garden was a theatre of response, and from the very beginnings of commentary on its various creations attention to design gave way increasingly to concern for reception. In England, Thomas Whately and Joseph Heely are fascinating in this respect, as are Hirschfeld in Germany and Claude-Henri Watelet in France.

Whately signals a transition in that his *Observations on Modern Gardening* of 1770 contains both instructional, design advice and narratives of affective response; his ekphrastic passages – a considerable chunk of the whole book – are dedicated to describing the impact of garden scenes or 'pictures' on notional visitors. Seven years later, Heely's *Letters on the Beauties of The Leasowes, Hagley and Enville* are tilted much more towards reception; his choice of epistles as the form of presentation – friend writing to friend – allows a more immediate and intimate narrative of garden experience in these three famous sites. And we will see the same shifts of emphasis on the continent: Watelet, especially in the epistolary section of his *Essai sur les jardins* of 1774, is primarily concerned to enunciate the rich symphony of response to garden scenes, which he even classifies by the kinds of appeal they will make. That Hirschfeld relied much on Watelet's little book is no surprise, since, despite his concern to give design principles and practical advice on layout for new German gardens, a major concern was to study affective responses: 'the essence of Hirschfeld's idea of the garden', writes his modern American translator, 'lies in the experience of it, in the ways it responds to us and to our expectations'.[20]

There is undoubtedly a rich body of material for a reception history of gardens to be discovered during the progress of Picturesque gardening. Perhaps simply because there was so much of it at that time, we are liable to overlook the existence of responses to garden experience before the eighteenth century. In an attempt to demonstrate the pervasive interest in garden reception in a wide variety of times and places, later essays here will look at both an early narrative of garden experience, the *Hypnerotomachia Poliphili* of 1499, and the ways in which Louis XIV's Versailles provoked a variety of contemporaries to track its specific impact on visitors who were both *au fait* with and strangers to its culture.

Indeed, it could be argued that garden art is uniquely characterized, indeed even constituted, by its endemic concern for how visitors will respond to it, its spaces and imagery being designed precisely to elicit reactions to the ensemble. Shakespeare may not – according to Matthew Arnold – 'abide our question', but gardens provoke them and, so to speak, stop to engage in discussion with their visitors. When Henry Peacham wished to praise the sculpture garden created by the Earl of Arundel beside the River Thames in the early seventeenth century he wrote of how its assemblage and positioning of Classical artefacts might 'persuade a man, that he now seeth two thousand years ago'; its revival of 'old Greece' was by design also a provocation of its visitors' responsive memories.[21]

v

In assembling for this book a selection of my writings, and more particularly in revising them for this volume, I was struck by how much my own interests have always focused without my knowing on what I now want to call reception rather than design history. As its title implies, my *Garden and Grove: The Italian Renaissance*

Garden in the English Imagination (1988) concerned, not the design of Italian gardens *per se*, but the experience of designed sites in Italy by visiting Englishmen and women throughout the seventeenth and early eighteenth centuries. This book in its turn had grown out of another, a study of the rise of the English landscape garden that resisted conventional design histories of that famous type of gardening. *The Figure in the Landscape: Poetry, Painting and Gardening during the Eighteenth Century* (1978), as that earlier book was called, discussed as much responses to landscape as the forms it took in designed work; poetry and painting were invoked there as much for their record of responses and experience as for their documentation of design history. I looked then for the meanings (metaphors or figures) that eighteenth-century people discovered in their landscapes; although I did not, I think, register it clearly in this way, what interested me then was those figures, not the shape of the ground.

One other personal direction has clearly influenced the desire to bring together these studies. For the last ten years I have taught the history and theory of landscape in a graduate school that trains professional landscape architects (also architects, planners and artists). Such students are, self-evidently, primarily concerned with their thinking and creativity as designers. But I was increasingly struck and somewhat surprised by their relative lack of interest in how their projects, once realized, might be received. Perhaps rightly, they paid little heed to how their 'words' could be or would be modified in the guts of the living persons who might inhabit their designs if and when built. Students have inventive, intelligent and imaginative ways of arriving at their designs, and this often involved a narrative of how the design project had been devised and followed through;[22] this effectively marginalized attention to the probable afterlife of their proposals. Little attention was paid to how their work would be received once something like it was built. To be fair, this was not always at issue in academic design studios, where

the individual student's own response to the design was taken
as typical and sufficient. But the weight of attention and creative
involvement none the less went into the process of making, with
the potential afterlife of the project left unexplored. Yet once
these professional designers do come to engage with real situ-
ations in real offices, and if they are to be good enough then to
make remarkable work, that work will have to be received, indeed
remarked on, by people outside the design field: visitors, clients,
consumers, whoever would encounter those new landscapes
and however one wants to call them. It is indeed interesting
that there is no satisfactory word to describe those who receive
gardens and landscape as opposed to those, landscape architects
or garden designers, who make them. As a result of this situation
in which I found myself thinking and teaching, I turned more
deliberately to asking about the reception of designed work in
the past, because I hoped that it would give sufficient hints about
future reception, which by its very nature could not be known
and only projected. That explains this present book.

TWO

The Garden as Virtual Reality

If we anticipate using the idea of a virtual visitor in a history of garden reception, that is to say an imagined person palimpsestially constructed of changing viewpoints, each one restricted in itself, it will be worth asking first to what extent the garden itself can be a 'virtual reality'; this will in turn help to define the contrary sense in which gardens must also be recognized as physical realities to which our virtual visitor might respond.

I

The term 'virtual reality' is an increasingly familiar and potent one in the twenty-first century. 'Virtual' has generally meant 'almost'; but (at least in American English) has surrendered its role as qualification in favour of being an intensifier – 'it's a virtual reality' meaning 'it's a strong reality, stronger than one would elsewhere encounter', even 'it has the virtue of reality'. It implies that through digital imagery we can gain access to imaginary or physically inaccessible worlds so effectively that we might as well be there in person; that they are so real that we interact with them as we would – or even more than we usually do – in real life. For instance, computer games like the CD-ROM game of MYST led us into a landscape where we were called on to make complicated decisions in navigating its territory.[1] Or in *Paul Cézanne:*

33

Portrait of my World[2] we could enter that painter's studio and, clicking on any of the objects scattered there, penetrate further the time capsule of his life and living.

There are also digital landscapes for our exploration. Rather than visit the actual resting place of a beloved's remains in a suburban cemetery and lay flowers on the grave, the World Wide Web now offers a virtual memorial garden, a resting place in cyberspace where you may post your memorials and leave your tokens of remembrance.[3] There is a digital Museum of Garden History (http://www.museumgardenhistory.org). And increasingly landscape architectural offices give clients the chance to explore in both cyberspace and cybertime their as yet unbuilt garden or property, seeing the growth of trees and shrubs over 10, 20 and 50 year periods, for instance, or seeing a site with and without specific features (illus. 9).[4]

Digital spatial modelling also offers enormous opportunities for the treatment of the conservation of historical sites. What has hitherto involved expensive reconstruction, often destructive of unnoticed evidence or evidence only recognized as such too late, can now be tried out and 'experienced' on the computer screen. What had been dangerously positivistic in prescription and reified permanently on a reconstructed site can now be enjoyed in digital format and, furthermore, a series of optional restorations can be available for the virtual visitor's enjoyment and adjudication. Projections of what a garden was or might have been can be augmented and modified at will, leaving the actual site free of costly and maybe distracting and destructive interventions.[5] This can be an especially potent tool when a garden has undergone many changes and its site is composed of palimpsestial, onion skins of history, each of which is worth recovering. The Tuileries Gardens in Paris would be a good example: their modern history involves interventions by André Mollet, then Le Nôtre and again by others at almost every stage in the development of the adjacent Louvre palace, including the

modern insertion of the I. M. Pei pyramids, all of which makes particularly difficult, even absurd, any decision as to what period a restoration should return the adjacent gardens. Recently the Tuileries were in fact 'restored' with a postmodernist bricolage of garden gestures designed by Jacques Wirtz, from which I suspect visitors derive little satisfaction and which certainly tells them nothing about the succeeding stages of the site's long history. An alternative proposal, by Bernard Lassus, actually adopted a strategy that was digitally devised, emphasizing quite literally the different historical layers and re-creating appropriate gardens at each level, so that visitors would be responding to the development of the site over several centuries as well as arriving, on the highest level next to the River Seine, at a platform treated in some modern style.[6] This proposal seems to have emanated precisely from a virtual strategy, as its presentation imagery suggested (illus. 10).

10 Bernard Lassus, 1992 proposal for the reinvention of the Tuileries Gardens, Paris, showing the different historical layers that would be brought to the surface and recreated.

II

But I do not intend here to explore the virtual reality of gardens in cyberspace, which must be left to those with more digital competence;[7] I suspect it must also wait until the potentialities of the technology have been explored and exploited more systematically, and digital imagery can fashion the materials of landscapes as convincingly as it can represent architectural work on the screen.

Instead, I want to pursue the idea of the physical garden itself as a virtual reality. For one way of thinking about landscape architecture is to emphasize the way in which it affords visitors many of the same opportunities as do sites on a computer screen: digitally, the visitor may choose his or her route, clicking on the mouse and opting for a variety of different paths, different experiences, different associations and ideas. Visiting a real site entails much of the same process, although now the 'mouse' is a person's deliberate or instinctive selection of routes and meanings within the one territory; this is especially true of a site as densely ordered as Versailles, with as many routes and interpretations today as there are visitors (to be sure, some routes and inter-pretations will be more plausible or compelling than others). This kind of visitation of a real garden also involves constant interac-tion of the subject and object, since the exploration of a real landscape is by no means a passive activity; even a small urban square requires us to 'get to know it', with its elements directing our growing acquaintance with its potential as a space to inhabit.

In this way all good landscape architecture also manages to project a sense both of reality and of virtuality. There is the palpable, haptic place, smelling, sounding, catching the eye (see illus. 12); then there is also the sense of an invented or special place, this invention resulting from the creation of richer and fuller experiences than would be possible, at least in such com-pleteness or intensity, if they were not designed. Like cyberspace, a designed landscape is always at bottom a fiction, a contrivance – yet its hold on our imagination will derive, paradoxically, from the actual materiality of its invented sceneries.

Landscape architecture is no stranger to paradox, although some of its practitioners seem fearful of such complexity. Among its least analysed paradoxes is precisely its 'virtual reality' – this combination of a felt experience of both organic and inorganic materials with a deliberate creation of fictive worlds into whose inventions, systems and mythological or metaphorical

languages we allow ourselves to be drawn. A garden is nothing if it does not thus seduce us; it is equally nothing of it does not insist on its own tangible existence. Even the most inorganic 'garden', like Isamu Noguchi's Beinecke Courtyard at Yale University (illus. 11), strongly declares its physical nature – the hardness, whiteness, clarity, even the austerity (the lack of smell) of its marble – before we begin to consider its virtual existence, its symbolism or the role it plays in a rare book library.

Not all gardens are as abstract or residual as this one. It is, however, difficult to find their sensual presences invoked in analyses of landscape architectural sites, especially historical sites, where admittedly that evidence could be very fragile; but it is equally difficult to know exactly how to invoke this empirical evidence. None the less, sometimes it is important to be able to do so. Since I intend to explore the past and the future potential of the garden as a *virtual* reality, I need also to recall how strongly its actualities work on us. And to underline how this too is paradoxical: the strong sensual, physical presence of things is both the means by which its imaginary zones are created or mediated and the brake on our total absorption in them.

In the very first Dumbarton Oaks symposium in 1971, that brilliant, exciting and not a little eccentric scholar Eugenio Battisti began by playing a tape of a garden visit — feet crunched on gravel, birds sang, other sounds came and went, water especially exhibited a whole repertoire of aquatic sounds, and there were significant pauses as time elapsed between acoustical events. Of course, it probably lacked the haptic rub of the hand along stone balustrades; certainly the smell of pine tree or the taste of refreshing water in the mouth on a hot Italian afternoon. When his learned and philosophical lecture on changing Renaissance ideas of nature was published, this tape was relegated to a mention in a footnote (in those days this was probably inevitable; nowadays perhaps a CD-ROM could accommodate its multi-medial contributions to Battisti's argument).[8]

A garden loses an essential part of its being and therefore an essential element of its significance in our discussions if we forget its smells, sounds and other, usually transient assaults on our senses and nervous system. Images that I took, say, of Anne's Grove in County Cork, Ireland (illus. 12), will have little impact without an accompanying sense of a lush, steaming, humid river

12 Anne's Grove, near Castletownroche, Co. Cork, Éire.

bottom in bright sun after torrential August showers, or the effort
of pushing through the overgrowth, as well as the sensation of
visiting a site, the scope, extent and significance of which were
essentially elusive at least for a first-time visitor. The wholly
insistent moment by moment changes in light on different surfaces or the altering focus of our sight (now distant, now close
up; now straight ahead, now alert to lateral possibilities that
our cameras will never catch[9]), let alone the different seasonal
changes in garden experience – this collective, visceral impact on
us during actual garden visits should shape all our accounts of
them; I suspect it rarely does. However, its impact on other
garden experiences that we can and do talk about is no less
important for being generally forgotten. I want to retain this
'reality check' throughout the next section of my discussion.

III

What kind of constructions and effects in landscape architecture
draw a visitor into the experience of the spaces and realities of a
site? By what process is his or her absorption in the site effected?
Is absorption, indeed, a desired product of garden visits? I cannot
think of a worthwhile garden or park into which I do not step –
on even the umpteenth visit – without a strong sense of entering
a special zone. This liminal experience, which anthropologists
have much discussed,[10] is heightened simply by the presence of
a palpable entrance: whether this is simply the act of stepping
through the iron gateways of the Jardin du Luxembourg from
the Boulevard St Michel, or the literal *rite de passage* of inter-
minable corridors and stairs in the bowels of the Villa d'Este
before emerging on its uppermost terrace (as the modern visitor
is required to do). It can be sudden, as stepping through an
opening into some high-walled enclosure invisible from the outside, or prolonged, as when we approach via some tree-lined

avenue. The English designer Humphry Repton was particularly
concerned with how people navigated his newly designed properties, where gate lodges and carefully conducted carriage drives
and / or pathways would announce the special place to which
they led. It is not a concern always feasible for modern property
owners, where the exigencies of cars or handicapped access
often frustrate the experience of a proper approach. But equally
often, it is just sheer lack of regard for this most important of
garden experiences: we can all think of examples of great places
spoilt by their modern approaches – the disaster imposed on
Bomarzo, with its shoddy cafeterias, shops and petting zoo;
even more elegantly designed interpretation centres, such as that
at Gunston Hall in Virginia, effectively spoil by deflecting (at
least my) concentration on arrival. Sir Henry Wotton in the
early seventeenth century, perhaps even referring to the Villa
d'Este, recognized the significance of this archetypal moment
of entry into gardens when he wrote of having seen 'a garden
(for the manner perchance incomparable) into which the first
access was a high walk like a terrace, from whence might be
taken a general view of the whole plot below but rather in a
delightful confusion, than with any plain distinction of the pieces
. . .'. But this moment of entry or liminal sensation would be
nothing if it were not immediately sustained and augmented by
the apprehension of design, order and purpose throughout the
site being visited, as the continuation of Wotton's remarks reveals:
'From this [terrace] the beholder descending many steps, was
afterwards conveyed again, by several mountings and valings
[i.e., descents], to various entertainments of his scent and sight . . .
every one of these diversities was as if he had been magically
transported into a new garden.'[11] Rather than finding his own
way, the garden seems to 'convey' (i.e., lead) him by routes that
were contrived ('many steps') precisely to involve him and other
visitors in its 'entertainments'. This theatrical metaphor, especially
given the contemporary interactive court spectacles, masques and

intermezzi with which Wotton was familiar and to which he is surely appealing here, further implies the visitors' involvement as spectators / actors; he makes clear, too, how much he was caught up into its excitements, absorbed in the magical domain of the Villa d'Este.

The Renaissance garden (illus. 13) was able to contrive this magical world partly through sheer novelty – ever more and more sophisticated hydrology, Herculean earth-moving, sculptural programmes of greater and greater intricacy, concentration and diversity of effects, even a botanical repertoire that caught the beholder up in amazement and awe that reflected back – along with the whole ensemble – on the patron or creator of the garden. The sixteenth century even invented a term – third nature – for this garden world to distinguish it from both the second nature of the cultural landscape (fields, urban developments and infrastructure) and the first world of unmediated nature or wilderness.[12]

13 Gustave Utens, lunette painting of the Medici villa at Pratolino, 1590s, oil on canvas.

The western European garden at its best never lost this need to work on its visitors and to transport them into a new experience (illus. 14), although the means at its disposal and the relative successes of their effects changed radically during the next three and half centuries. In this we ask surely no more of a garden than of a novel or a piece of music: we want to be caught up in its world, however much our analytical skills remain alert to assess the reasons for such absorption. The verbal forms to express this absorption in garden art changed (inevitably), and by the nineteenth century the self-confessedly 'poetical' language of Henry Wotton[13] declined to a mere sentimental effusion, largely directed at horticultural realities; as a result, our focus on the garden's hold over us was deflected.

14 Jean-Jacques de Boissieu, drawing of a garden scene, 1793.

Yet it is an essential element in the full experience of a landscaped site that we appreciate its distinctiveness, its endemic separation from other worlds however ambiguous may be its boundaries, its effort at being different. Traditionally, there have been various strategies employed to achieve this. The most usual consists of a concentration of effects within the site – whether botanical, arboricultural, sculptural, aquatic or spatial. Another involves the abstraction or epitomizing of natural and cultural worlds outside the site, what earlier garden makers called 'representation' – as, for instance, John Worlidge in 1669 writing that 'Gardens, orchards, parterres, avenues . . . represent unto us epitomized, the form and idea of the more ample and spacious pleasant fields, groves and other rustic objects'.[14] Even in the so-called English landscape garden, where conspicuous artistic effects tended to be eliminated, the studied manipulation of organic elements – terrain, water, trees (not to mention the ways in which we are made aware of the sky) – alerts visitors to the special zone into which they have penetrated. In even the most naturalistic of modern ecological designs (illus. 15), it is precisely

15 The Crosby Arboretum, Picayune, Mississippi, designed by Ed Blake and Andropogon.

the design that tells of the studied return of the site to an idea of original purity and natural diversity.

The learned discussion of garden iconography, narrative structures and meaning in landscape architecture has tended to dominate its historiography. Yet this rarely addresses the question of how all that apparatus and a priori knowledge were available to and impacted on visitors, even ignoring the extent to which the recovered iconography was accessible to contemporaries as it can be made to be so by modern scholars for their students. Indeed, iconographical explanations of gardens are often flawed or (more honestly) frustrated precisely because there is no visitor evidence to collaborate their perspectives – Bomarzo is a case in point, since it is also a site where reception outweighs, indeed over-determines, iconographical explanations.[15] I think that we can deduce from careful study, say, of English visitors' responses to Italian gardens that their range of interest and therefore the intricacy and extent of their absorption extended way beyond mere iconographical event and narrative.[16] We know, for instance, how fascinated travellers were with hydraulic effects, and that their discovery of the precise mechanisms that produced them did nothing to diminish their enchantment with their metamorphic play. The often laborious, though none the less rewarding, exegeses of programmes for the Villa d'Este, the Labyrinth at Versailles and the Elysian Fields at Stowe – to take three well-researched sites – are generally unable to explain how people actually engaged in the decipherment of the narratives.[17] For Stowe, we do have the extremely useful *Dialogue* by the young William Gilpin; its construction as a dialogue usefully dramatizes two different kinds of response – the enthusiastic appreciation of effects in one speaker, the problem-solving and analytical instinct of the other. If we could find systematic ways to invoke and analyse paintings and other graphic works that show garden visitors in the process of exploration, we might have additional evidence of the kinds of hold that gardens had on them.

What is interesting, however, about Gilpin's account is that he shows the garden visitor as 'interactive', choosing his route, voicing his preferences, getting more or less involved at each junction. In landscapes where *fabriques* were beginning to be designed in a variety of styles – Classical, Gothic, Chinese, Turkish, Swiss or what-have-you – the opportunities for such interaction were arguably more varied if not greater. Yet are they any different in kind, rather than in the degree and quality of the interactions proposed, from the decipherment of mythic quotation and allusion or the response to technology and spectacle in earlier Renaissance gardens or at the Versailles of Louis xiv? Just because such a wholly different guide to Gilpin's as Louis xiv's *Manière de montrer les jardins de Versailles* does not reveal 'interactivity', should we assume that it did not take place?[18]

IV

Have gardens at some periods rather than others offered visitors more opportunity to immerse themselves in an imaginary world? Or is it simply that the records available to us privilege different modes of response and involvement? The gardens of Monceau (illus. 16), designed for the Duc de Chartres by Carmontelle in the 1770s, were also published by their designer in a *recueil* of 1779 at the termination of the work.[19] This publication makes clear that for Carmontelle, even more than for, say, William Chambers in England, gardens were above all a question of scenography, in which society could enjoy, amuse and involve itself. In a famous paragraph he wrote:

Why should one refuse to make of a Picturesque garden a territory of illusion? It is with illusions alone that we amuse ourselves: if liberty guides them, art directs and nature is

16 Louis Carrogis, called Carmontelle, *The Artist Presenting the Keys of the Jardin Monceau to the Duc de Chartres*, c. 1778, oil on canvas.

never too far away. Nature is various according to climates: let us try, by illusionary means, to vary the climate, or rather to forget the one where we find ourselves; let us transport into our gardens the changes of scene from the Opera; let us make in reality what clever scene-painters can offer in decoration, all times and all places. We must be allowed to avoid that cold monotony, produced by so-called strict precepts, that constrains the imagination. Since everything must be created, let us use that liberty to please, amuse and be interesting. That's what those who came to the Monceau Garden counted on finding; since they said, when there were few things [to absorb them in a garden], they'd prefer to walk in the country. What they expected to find here, then, was what ordinarily they'd not encounter.[20] [my translation]

This is as eloquent a claim for the virtual reality of landscape architectural invention that I know; despite the problematic degree of seriousness we need to impute to Carmontelle – was he simply enjoying himself in the creation of all those illusionary times and places or was he offering a solemn masonic itinerary? – he clearly

capitalizes on the garden's by now established potential for
virtual reality.

There are other sites – we can all think of examples – where
the creation of new spaces was intended to enthral. The Buttes-
Chaumont in Paris (illus. 17), perhaps more than the southern
end of Olmsted's Central Park in New York, fabricates a world
of impressive natural features: vertiginous cliffs stripped of their
vegetation in order to enhance that sublimity, caverns and waterfalls. These events are accessed by carefully determined paths
and high slung bridges (technologically modern, of a piece with
the railway line that was allowed to retain its place in the park
ensemble); these elements of 'wilderness' that allude to the
previous uses of the site for hangings and criminal punishments
are also side by side with boating facilities, cafés and some
marvellously pastoral gradings of the slopes. These contrasts and
contradictions only make it more obvious that this is a palpably
invented and artificially varied landscape. Yet the illusions – the
virtualities – of the Buttes-Chaumont are surely fuelled both by
our sense of them as faked or feigned and by the palpable realities

18 Concrete rails, imitating wood, in the Buttes-Chaumont park, Paris.

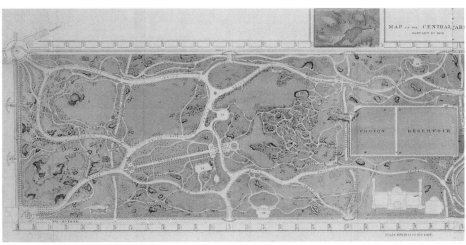

19 Calvert Vaux and Jacob Mould's plan of Central Park, detail of a coloured lithograph published in 1869. The Ramble is immediately to the left of the reservoir.

of rock, water, earth: the false wooden railings, so rustic, yet fabricated in concrete or *rocaille* (illus. 18), are symbolic of the whole and of our paradoxical response to it.

By comparison, Central Park's picturesque Ramble (illus. 19), by aiming to represent a less extreme 'nature' and by utilizing a less extreme site in the first place (though none the less adhering to and enhancing the geological givens), promotes a very different effect. I myself prefer the Buttes-Chaumont precisely because its promotion of illusion is both more intense and more obvious – I respond to its 'virtual reality'; but there is no doubt that Central Park also offers to many thousands of visitors, generation after generation, the illusion of wilderness or natural scenery that is probably the stronger for not drawing attention to its fabrication.

The creation of absorbing zones can be total and encompassing as well as expensive; but it can also work through the most minimal means. An example of the first, now no longer visitable,

20 The Crowninshield Garden near Hagley, Delaware, *c.* 1981.

was the Crowninshield Garden in Delaware on the banks of the Brandywine River (illus. 20). Created for a member of the wealthy Dupont family in the 1920s, the site is the terraced hillside of a former gunpowder factory; but that industrial ruin was, bizarrely, enhanced by a neo-Classical scenography out of Cecil B. De Mille. Columns, mosaic pavements, busts and marble stairs turned the site into an ancient Roman dreamscape. Once completed, work-men were apparently sent in with sledgehammers to break up the new installations, to turn it into a ruin. It was, when I saw it – seventeen years ago – magical in exactly the way that the Crowninshields must have wanted, an 'instant' ruined Roman garden, with which the industrial remains of the saltpetre works somehow cohabited in ways that enhanced the idea of the ruined garden at the same time as they called attention to its *pays d'illusion*.[21]

At the other extreme from the expense and labour of the Crowninshield Garden is the work of the Montreal-based artist, Gilbert Boyer, whose interventions (though doubtless not cheap) are far less wholesale. Recent installations have involved the insertion into existing space – the grassland of the Olmstedian Mount Royal in Montreal itself (illus. 21), house walls in the town of Aulnoy-les-Valenciennes in northern France – of what purport to be messages, letters or references to books. Letters are essentially an interactivity (we write them, send them, open them, read them, respond to them); Boyer invites us to read and respond to these dispersed letters, imagining from their scattered fragments the histories of unknown personal lives. Throughout Aulnoy are scattered 46 glass discs, 60 cm in diameter, which Boyer calls 'Addresses personnelles'; they connect sites to books, so that the usually passive act of reading is transformed into an interactive adventure; references interconnect, taking one from the municipal library to other parts of town and from there back into books, bits of which address one from their walls, yet give the library call number as a further reference. The series has the possibility of infinite extension.[22]

V

With the work of Gilbert Boyer, unlike Crowninshield or the Buttes-Caumont, we are in the contemporary world of minimal interventions, suitably geared for an ecological age that is sceptical of intrusion into what is deemed the 'natural' world (although that is not, I believe, Boyer's motive). But it leads to a final consideration, not just of the historical dimension of the garden as virtual reality, but to its future potential in that mode.

Clearly, the history of landscape architecture sustains sufficiently the claim that gardens have been what Carmontelle called *pays d'illusion*, virtual realities, although (necessarily) the precise scope of both realities and virtualities is different at different times and places. Medieval to modern sites have been created in the expectation that they would absorb their visitors, enthral or envelop them in their imaginary worlds, yet firmly ground them (literally) in a world of palpable physical dimensions: from gardens as playgrounds of courtly rites of love, about which the poets endlessly sang their astonishment, to William Kent's Rousham, a confection of exquisite scale and tonality where the Classical past is connected to fresh localities and customs; from that wondrous romance, the *Hypnerotomachia Poliphili* of 1499, to the parks and even café décor that Giuseppe Jappelli, skilled in illusionary scenography, made the sites of personal and political transformations.[23]

Now the potential of this central aspect of garden art does not, indeed cannot, lie in the endless restoration or even conservation of former *pays d'illusion*. The twenty-first century has its own illusions and needs to invent their appropriate territories. Personally I think we rush too quickly to restore or conserve far too many old sites, instead of exploring new ways of inventing the past; sometimes their recovery would be impossible physically, but more often we can never contrive the same mind sets that would have responded to them originally. As suggested already, digital modelling lends itself to reconstructions of historical sites that are less costly, less destructive and less prescriptive than site-specific work; this in its turn opens more doors to contemporary landscape architecture, only in very recent years willing to face its future and resume traditional responsibilities of invention as opposed to conservation.

Carmontelle was not wrong to say that we live with and by illusions, and landscape architecture is, at least in part, in the business of providing these virtual realities. His determination to transfer the skills of scene-painters from the theatre to gardens was something that Baudelaire, in arguing for the excitements and necessities of modernism, also invoked; but for Baudelaire the scene-painters were liars because they did not lie enough![24] He wanted less literal, less ordinary landscapes in which the theatre of modern life could perform; scene-painters were liars because for him they failed to perform this greater truth. In *As You Like It*, Shakespeare's fool, Touchstone, had offered the same wisdom: 'The truest poetry is the most feigning.' Landscape architecture needs to recover this venerable tradition in artistic production.

However, more Disneyworlds, more theme parks, are not the answer either, though this is not to deny what is presumably their compelling hold on the imaginations of many visitors. What is central to the success of such places, however, though it is not necessarily stated by their creators and promoters in this way, is the invention of places, invention that carries with it that paradoxical quality of utter conviction (founded on physical construction) with acknowledgement of its illusion (to which the physical constructs also contribute).

It is a conviction of some modern landscape architecture practice that sites are to be reinvented. By this is meant not just putting historical sites back 'as they were', which largely neglects the important consideration that we, the modern consumers, no longer receive or are absorbed in the same way as were our ancestors in places like Stowe, Monceau or Versailles; but reinvention means rather to refashion for a modern consumption that needs to encounter a past that may be wholly fictional, like Bernard Lassus's Jardin de l'Antérieur with its 'legendary' *meer* emitting 'prehistoric' noises (illus. 22), or creatively transformed, as with the same artist's proposals for the Tuileries site or his

built Garden of Returns in the Parc de la Corderie Royale at
Rochefort-sur-Mer. If these projects largely reinvent a narrative
out of the given materials of moribund sites – one of the characteristic strategies of some of our best designers today – other
initiatives deploy more formal means, playful reorderings that
transfigure organic and inorganic materials: Peter Walker's Tanner
Fountain outside Harvard Yard (illus. 23), or Lawrence Halprin's
fountains in Portland, Oregon. Narratively – that is to say either
historically angled, or simply offering us fresh versions of the
present moment – these are all places literally made over into
fabulous ground.

This, finally, returns us to an essential difference between the
creations of landscape architecture and the virtual realities of
digital media. The uniqueness of landscape architecture consists
in our being able to walk through a site, opening ourselves to the

22 Bernard Lassus,
Le Jardin de
l'Antérieur, 1975.

myriad sensations that it generates. This is a far cry from even the most absorbing virtual reality available to us sitting still with headphones in front of a screen. Landscape architecture may not be able to afford in future to intervene in actual sites so as to contrive realities that match the brave new world of digital imaging; but whatever its limitations, it still realizes (literally) what it invents. Those people who are professionally and therefore centrally concerned with landscape architecture must ensure that it does not abandon its skills and creative vision, its invention of worlds to absorb us whenever we cross their thresholds.

THREE

Experiencing Gardens and Landscapes in the *Hypnerotomachia Poliphili*

I

If we are inclined to think that early, regular or what are sometimes termed 'formal' gardens did not promote much concern for how they were experienced, but instead were valued both then and later for their design, their formal achievements, then some early texts suggest otherwise. In the journal of his travels in Italy Michel de Montaigne records not just items that he saw in gardens there, but his own reactions to, his experience of them. He writes, about his visit to Pratolino, of the Medici duke's exercise of 'all his natural five senses in embellishing' the site and of his own equally full response that goes beyond merely graphic description. At another Medici property, Castello, he notices what he calls 'a natural-looking artificial rock', a phrase that clearly suggests how he is concerned to interpret his impressions of this intricate play between nature and artifice that were such a prized feature of these places.[1] Similarly, the Modenese artist Giovanni Guerra, touring some of the same gardens a little later in the sixteenth century to research the latest developments in garden art, often added captions to his sketches as a means of enhancing their record not just of formal designs but of how they struck him (illus. 24).[2]

But the most interesting case of an early fascination with the experience of gardens comes in that intriguing and mysterious romance, probably written and certainly published in Venice in 1499, the *Hypnerotomachia Poliphili*, or, as it was called in a partial

24 Giovanni Guerra,
The Pegasus Fountain,
Bomarzo, c. 1598,
pen and ink drawing
with wash.

L'ORDINE DEL FONTE CABALINO DI BVONMARTIO
CONTIENE OLTRE ALLE MVSE NELLI QVATRO ANGOLI FVOR
DEL GIRO FIGVRA DI GIOVE APOLO BACCO E MERCVRIO

English translation of 1592, *The Strife of Love in a Dream.*[3] Yet such
is the fascination with only formal matters of design that even
this narrative of a lover's wanderings through a series of strange
and enigmatic sceneries, where he is constantly challenged as to
their meanings and significance, has been hailed for its concern
with design: thus Robert Harbison writes of how the object, the
finished object, is put at the centre of this book, and he contrasts
this focus with that of a gothic novel like *The Mysteries of Udolpho,*
where the process of appreciation is more central than the form

of the objects themselves.[4] But this emphasis is surely wrong, and perhaps derives from too much attention by critics like Harbison to the architectural structures that Poliphilo discovers[5] and too little interest in the landscapes; for the experience of both designed and found landscapes by the dreaming subject, Poliphilo, is very much at the core of Francesco Colonna's work. The author displays, indeed, a sustained and absorbed concern with how subject–object relationships lie at the heart of garden experience. So, against the prejudice, too often conveyed, that the interest of 'formal' gardens lies in their objects and forms rather than in the process of their visitation, a corrective can be offered via an examination of the *Hypnerotomachia Poliphili* (all the while admitting that some of its forms have, especially via their illustrations, inspired several actual and painted garden designs, from the arcade in Mantegna's *Virtue Driving Vice from the Garden* in the Louvre to Mansart's Colonnade at Versailles and perhaps the wisteria arbour at Dumbarton Oaks in Washington, DC).

The richness not to say ambiguity of this work, however, also involves our experience as readers of its text, which both parallels and complicates the protagonist's reading of the landscapes. Poliphilo's narrative of his dream within a dream is filtered through a text at once intricately and inventively verbal and visual. It is, though, not simply that we read a tale that has been illustrated; but that the words re-present experiences that the published imagery also reflects apparently directly. There is, of course, no way in which the visual record can be said to be Poliphilo's, as is a plausible case for the verbal narrative, which, by contrast, suggests a more intimate relation between text and protagonist. None the less the *mise-en-page* of the first (as indeed of subsequent editions) creates a strange illusion of the author permitting Poliphilo the double perspective of verbal and visual by which to fix or triangulate and articulate the objects that he experiences. Hence the constant changefulness of how the illustrations are selected, placed and used both within a given edition and throughout the different published versions – sometimes alongside the relevant text, sometimes delayed briefly or held back for long periods; here carefully glossed, there presented without significant commentary. Our navigation of the book as readers is therefore in some insistent fashion an implied analogue to Poliphilo's need to understand his journey through different landscapes.

It is also important to recall how gardens were themselves similarly composed of both verbal and visual experiences. Inscriptions, as a later essay here explores, have been a fundamental aspect of garden art, and even when they seemed to go out of fashion it was still a customary expectation of garden visits that visual sightings would often be translatable into words. Reflections and reactions, either conscious or unconscious, immediate or delayed, shared with companions or stored in the mind for later communication, all need words to articulate them fully.

This makes a further and final preliminary point: that the *Hypnerotomachia Poliphili* relies on what seems to be a studied concern for and familiarity with garden experience. It is not, then, simply a literary fantasy, but draws on garden experience in a way that we can study profitably as if it were, like Mme de Scudéry's *Promenade de Versailles*, about an actual place. We have no idea what kinds of gardens, real or imaginary, were known to the author of the book, although he must have read (I suspect) other literary descriptions of similar scope: the French medieval poem *Le Roman de la rose* is also about how a person navigates a series of garden spaces and learns from his experiences in them; garden *ekphraseis* in Byzantine prose romances would be another plausible 'source' or model for the author, and here too the verbal description both rendered visual events (the usual thrust of an *ekphrasis*) and articulated the more inward elements of garden experience.[6] Nor do we have to be purely historical: Colonna's book can reap the benefits of its own afterlife, just as it is argued in other essays here that actual gardens do, and we should ensure that our reading of this romance also makes a wide appeal to a

relevant variety of subsequent garden imagery and experience at
Pratolino, Bomarzo, the Hortus Palatinus in Heidelberg, the
Recepte véritable of Bernard Palissy, the designs of Jacques Androuet
du Cerceau, even Mansart's Colonnade at Versailles or the wisteria
arbour at Dumbarton Oaks. Acquaintance with some of those
will help us, even anachronistically, to appreciate better the garden
experiences of Poliphilo.

II

Almost every analysis of the *Hypnerotomachia Poliphili* chooses to
retell the story or details of its plot – an eloquent demonstration
of our need to re-make or experience the narrative as our own.
Here I plan to omit these *de rigueur* synopses, not to pretend to
any more objective reading, but simply to focus on what concerns
us. The dreamer has many experiences of different landscapes
and gardens, spread over five distinct zones or topographies,
which have been usefully and legibly mapped by Gilles Polizzi
(illus. 25).[7] The first of these is the dark forest and the shady
riverbank, in each of which he falls asleep and starts to dream
(the second time dreaming within his first dream!); mountains
apparently intervene before the second landscape, comprising
another plain and wood, with a fantastic pyramid; then after
more mountains he comes to the third, consisting of a plain,
a river spanned by a bridge, more woodland through which he
moves to the intricate palace and gardens of Eleutherilide, after
which there is another river and bridge and his arrival at a triple
set of doorways; the fourth landscape comprises yet another
plain, woods with trellis structures, pageants that are presented
in an orchard, and other architectural features; his fifth and final
landscape experience takes place in the circular gardens of
Cythere, at the very centre of which is the amphitheatre and
fountain of Venus.

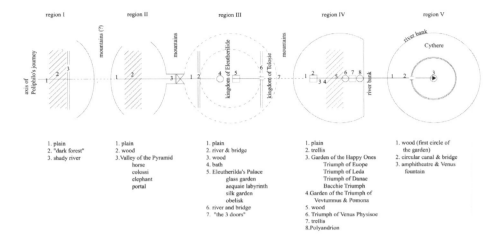

1. plain	1. plain	1. plain	1. plain	1. wood (first circle of
2. "dark forest"	2. wood	2. river & bridge	2. trellis	the garden)
3. shady river	3.Valley of the Pyramid	3. wood	3. Garden of the Happy Ones	2. circular canal & bridge
	horse	4. bath	Triumph of Euope	3. amphitheatre & Venus
	colossi	5. Eleutherilda's Palace	Triumph of Leda	fountain
	elephant	glass garden	Triumph of Danae	
	portal	aequaie labyrinth	Bacchie Triumph	
		silk garden	4.Garden of the Triumph of	
		obelisk	Vevtumnus & Pomona	
		6. river and bridge	5. wood	
		7. "the 3 doors"	6. Triumph of Venus Physisoe	
			7. trellis	
			8.Polyandrion	

25 Diagram of the topographical zones of the *Hypnerotomachia Poliphili* by Gilles Polizzi.

Poliphilo has different kinds of experience in these succeeding landscapes and gardens. The first to be registered is that it is only in retrospection that we understand fully what we have encountered; the reader is thus distinguished from Poliphilo, for whom such coherence is impossible.[8] Our attention is drawn specifically to this tension between local experience and the acquisition of an overall sense of place by Poliphilo's occasional anticipation of returning to parts that perplex him or his promise to himself to make such return visits (p. 32). Especially on a complex site, the relation of parts to whole is not an explanation or comprehension available to first-time visitors – short of sudden levitation to seize a bird's-eye view, a graphic formula for explaining sites that became of course hugely popular and important for gardens where the intricate detailing of parts could seduce the visitor from considering the whole. In fact, the extreme precision of each scene in the *Hypnerotomachia*, the extraordinarily haptic description of each sector, isolates that particular space and moment and, although preternaturally clear and explicit, its larger meaning can be baffling – in terms even of topographical situation, let alone other issues and themes. Poliphilo, like garden visitors generally, is not therefore able to pace or place himself appropriately, either in his movement or his thinking. He misjudges his position or even his route, thinking an end is in sight when it is not. In practice, experienced garden visitors, which Poliphilo is not allowed to be, suspend analysis, storing each section of the site in provisional *schemata*, until they have a sense of the whole (a whole that second, third or multiple visits could reshape). Poliphilo's necessary failure as a garden visitor requires that the reader will take on this overall role of probing the sequence of landscape architectural events; however, Colonna's own 'peculiar feeling for sequence' and for the additive function of accumulation, reflected in his acrostic acknowledgement of authorship, directs the reader's procedure.[9]

Poliphilo's journey takes him through a series of sites marked by a profusion of both artefacts and natural elements. It is only when he arrives at the circular gardens of Cythera, the final zone of the story, that some significance in his landscape journey begins to emerge; but it was initiated, in fact, at the very start of the story. This constitutes the second garden experience, which concerns, not surprisingly, the *paragone* of art and nature in garden-making and, by implication, the *paragone* of verbal and visual in understanding and describing that dialectic. After all, the Renaissance was nothing if not obsessed with the proper adjudication of the respective contributions and responsibilities of art and nature; in gardens such a comparison, rivalry or contest was especially well (fore)grounded, as Colonna is perfectly aware (and we, mired in an ecological positivism, are not).

The essential parameters of that *paragone* are set out in the opening sequence of the story, where Poliphilo enters and then leaves the wild wood, and then in the next territory or zone finds and explores the huge pyramid and its landscape; in other words, he experiences topographies with very different levels of intervention that necessarily focus his mind (and ours) on the ratio and significance of such artifice. This territory is not plotted for us – that kind of mapping is reserved for the last, circular garden of Cythera – and Poliphilo is forced to retrace his steps at least once, so random is or appears the site. Perhaps it is significant that this brings him twice to the statue of Pegasus, whose presence in many Renaissance gardens (e.g., Villa Lante, Bomarzo, Villa d'Este at Tivoli, see illus. 24) can be said to dramatize an aspect of the art / nature debate. A fountain with statuary re-enacts the mythical narrative of the winged horse striking the mountainside of Parnassus with his hoof and releasing the spring of the Muses, whose activity it is to mediate and re-present the real world through their arts, for which activity a garden is an especially appropriate place.

The landscape of the pyramid is marked by an abundance of natural forms, especially botanical specimens, but also including lizards (in this anticipating Bernard Palissy's ceramics[10]). Poliphilo is largely, but not exclusively, terrified or confounded by this fecundity: he tells us that his memory is confused with its variety, and his sight 'blurred with continual gazing'.[11] At another moment he thinks that the weeds, brambles and wild flowers – though lovingly listed and observed – are only 'hindering'[12] his seeing and understanding of the ruined fabric that they cover, an emblem of a disproportioned relation of nature and art. Yet there are other moments, necessarily less frequent at this stage, when the profusion is delightful and seems to declare human intervention so much that he looks around for a country house.[13] A spring of water presents itself in terms that in another context would adequately describe a fountain contrived in the naturalistic mode; except that here nature plays too obtrusive a role.[14]

Yet it is back to these same riches and variety of nature herself that works of art lead Poliphilo. He is quick to praise the mimetic possibilities of art ('surpassing imitation of nature'[15]) or to lament its frustrations, such as the inability of human figures in bas-reliefs to sing or to weep.[16] Indeed, it is the verbal supplement – the inscription of two words, TEMPVS (time) and AMISSIO (loss) – that draws attention to the carving's less-than-perfect imitation of temporal process.

It is towards the end of this sequence that the elder Pliny ('il naturale historico' [p. 50]) is invoked to praise the porch, presumably because this feature answers to the wide-ranging agenda of his *Natural History*. But the sequence ends with a series of *ekphraseis* of landscape paintings that represent 'Waters, Fountaines, Mountaines, Rilles, woodes, and beasts, in their natural coulours',[17] which links itself explicitly and etymologically to Pliny's proposals for a similar decoration of country houses. However, the triumph of verbal over (imagined) visual in the *ekphraseis* is matched by the paintings' visual supremacy over the natural sceneries that they represent; only in actual garden landscapes will verbal and visual collaborate and in the process transcend that rivalry. But that moment is deferred.

III

Its deferral, we will later realize, makes room for the next sequence in the realm of Queen Eleuterilyda, where Poliphilo is conducted through an extravagantly artful series of landscape architectures. Their astonishing invention is not in question; but their relationship with the natural worlds they mimic is – perhaps most clearly adumbrated in the English text by the description of the glass garden:

> The ground was here and there covered with great round balles of glasses lyke gunne stones, and other fine proportions much pleasing, with a mutuall consent unmooueable like pearles shining without any adulteration by solyat-ure. From the flowers did breath a sweet fragrancie by some cleare washing with oyle for that purpose.[18]

This glass garden, along with the three others in this territory, stretches the plausibility of garden representation to its limits:[19] botanical perfumes are faked, the Labyrinth substitutes water channels, negotiated by boats, for paths between its hedges;[20] in the third, trunks, branches, leaves and flowers are all crafted in 'fine silk, wanting no store of Pearles to beautify the same'.[21] Significantly, only the French edition tried to illustrate these three artful gardens (illus. 26), in the process inevitably making them seem more plausible by drawing (as the artist would have been forced to do) upon familiar imagery. Because French readers could in their turn have matched the illustrations with other available imagery (painted, printed, engraved, manuscript), the sense of exceptional and extraordinary artfulness is diminished. The original Italian and the English editions avoid – perhaps deliberately – imagery that by its very nature cannot commun-icate either the falsity of the similitudes (glass stones, silk foliage) or their formal devising; this strategy of omission forces readers, if not Poliphilo, to adjudicate these designs for themselves.

On several occasions Colonna nudges the reader to under-stand these matters aright: as when in the midst of the silk grass, leaves and flowers he makes Poliphilo tell of an Arbour con-structed of gold wire and 'overspread' with gold roses 'more beautiful to the eye, then if they had been growing roses'.[22] By contrast, surely not accidental, in the third zone Poliphilo will meet his love Polia for the first time under a similar pergola tunnel, which now is illustrated not once but twice in the Venice text (illus. 27); for all its carpenter's work, 'lifting uppe and bending over', it also flourishes 'with the pleasant and odiferous flowers of three sorts comixt [of jasmine]'.[23]

Poliphilo's appreciation of art and architecture has hitherto been linked conventionally to the clarity of its mediating role: 'for take away order and rule, and what thing can any man make, either beautiful to the eye, or of commendable proportion and durable'.[24] What he encounters in this seductive sequence, which

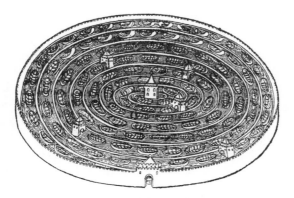

26 The three
artful gardens from
a French edition,
Le Songe de Polifile
(Paris, 1546).

27 One of the two
illustrations of the
pergola from the first
Venice edition of
*Hypnerotomachia
Poliphili* (1499).

is initiated with his bathing session with the nymphets and the
incident with the *Manneken-pisse*, is not so commended. Indeed,
it is preceded and followed (as we have just noticed) by scenic
incidents that encourage discrimination and suggest value through
a dual comparison: of one scenery with another, and of a
contrived, landscaped architecture with its 'model'.

Poliphilo enters into the realm of Eleuterilyda via a 'fayre and
plentiful countrie, fruitfull fieldes, and fertile groundes'.[25] This he
compares properly with the 'mountain unnaturall' out of which
he has just escaped, 'overgrowne and shaddowed' with many
(specified) trees. Indeed, this sequence of passage from one zone
well into the next is underscored with many such comparisons
and contrasts.[26] For in matters of such subtle discrimination

between art and nature, we need all possible occasions on which to test our skills. These manoeuvres are of a piece with the later humanist understanding of garden art as a third nature, distinguished by its complex collaboration of art and nature from the second nature of agrarian work or the wild woods and mountains in first nature.[27]

What the reader can do that Poliphilo does not is to compare this agrarian fertility and control with the silk and glass gardens ahead of him, for it is in this pleasant 'countrie' that he comes upon the eight-sided bathhouse and the Queen's seductive nymphs. Yet he himself, admiring the carving inside the bathhouse, is led to make comparisons between it and the thoroughly palpable nymphs – 'oftentimes my eyes would wander from the real and lively shapes, to looke upon those feyned representations'; immediately afterwards he also remarks how the fish represented in the bottom of the bathing pool 'did so imitate nature as if they had been swimming alive'.[28]

The silk and glass gardens are sufficiently contextualized in the narrative by two other descriptions of the Queen's palace (themselves involving contrasts): the courtyard garden before the palace, and Poliphilo's less localized review of the architectural amenities just before the ballet.[29] These are both extremely complex descriptions, but I think it is fair to say that they oppose natural amenities, well ordered and represented, to wholly artificial designs which are 'as uneasie to report as uncredible to beleeve': on the one hand, for instance, a latticework of branches ('not without a wonderful worke') framed into an arbour of the sort that would be illustrated in Crispijn van de Passe's *Hortus floridus* (1614); on the other, a courtyard where everything is worked in gold, down to the scale and spacing of individual leaves on a tapering branch. This is immediately followed, however, in Poliphilo's breathless celebration of the palace ensemble, with its antithesis:

delightful fruitfulness of the set hedges, Orchards, watered Gardens, springing Fountains, current streames in Marble channelles, conteined, framed, and held in, with an incredible Art, greene Herbes, full freshe and flowering, a sweet ayre, wartne and spring windes, with a confused chartne of singing and chirping birdes . . .[30]

The balance (even the 'confused charme') of artful ordering and natural ingredients anticipates, though it does not by any means match, the final perfection of garden art in Cythera's realm.

IV

However, Poliphilo has one more zone to travel before he arrives there. In so doing he enjoys, even on his way out of Eleuterilyda's territory, some new garden experiences that emphasize the intellect rather than the senses. From the silk garden the maiden Logistica (or Reason) leads him into another garden, this time encircled with ivy-covered, arched niches, and with a basin and obelisk at its centre. The verbal elucidation of this ensemble, itself composed of letters, artificial forms and natural materials, marks Poliphilo's advance into a better appreciation of spiritual matters. But significantly it also leads him to celebrate the physical garden where he takes his tutorial in metaphysics:

Where there breathed a sweet ayre from heaven, with unvariable wines, in this Garden round about full of flowers, of a large and circular permanent plot: compassed about with all sorts of fruites, pleasant in taste and full of health; with a perpetuall greenesse, disposed and set by a regular order, both beautiful, pleasant, and convenient; with the perfect labour and indevour of Nature to bring it to that passe, and beautified with precious gold.[31]

28 The Priapus
Fountain, from the
*Hypnerotomachia
Poliphili* (1499).

And this new awareness of gardenist skill prepares him and the
reader for the river landscape, the grove of plane trees and the
grotto-like doors in the side of the mountain.

The new experience of relating landscape to intellectual
matters seems to be the theme of this zone. After Poliphilo at
last meets Polia under the arbour, the lovers travel across an
indeterminately plotted and seemingly unmediated landscape,
where they encounter a whole series of allegorical, emblematical
and even 'actual' representations of mythical figures that all
concern human relations with the natural world; all these visual
experiences are carefully translated into verbal commentary. The
imagery includes a pastoral cast of deities of woods, mountains,
valleys and springs, triumphal cars bearing, among others,
Vertumnus and Pomona, and finally installations dedicated to

the two prime deities of gardens: the altar dedicated to Priapus, with its 'rude simulachro del' hortulano custode' (illus. 28),[32] followed soon afterwards by the circular Temple of Venus. The heavily interpretative session continues through Poliphilo's visit, now on his own, to a ruined temple by the shore and his laborious transcription and illustration of its many antique fragments (see illus. 31). Only with this antiquarian tutorial behind him, can he, together again with Polia, embark on their final voyage to the circular isle of Cythera, laid out as a series of concentric gardens.

V

This is probably the best known gardenscape of the book. Its elaborately described and imaged design constitutes the culmination, resolution and integration of all the preceding garden experiences, as Poliphilo himself in part realizes when he says that he compares it with those places he has previously seen.[33] And whatever arcane symbolism this sequence carries and however idealistic the garden, we cannot ignore that its scenery is very physical; the narrative needs and insists upon this palpable experience, which the attempt at a botanical reconstruction by Aga Segre helps us to understand more specifically.[34]

I will single out four main aspects of Cythera's garden that are of a different order than the horticultural on which Segre provides a commentary. First, it is mapped, or viewed overall; indeed, in a double sense Poliphilo surveys its totality – rhetorically in an opening description of highly generalized language,[35] then in his detailed topographical survey, by the end of which we realize that what we have been reading is offered before he and Polia disembark on the island and engage in any exploration of the site. During the subsequent local perambulations, in contrast, Poliphilo surrenders himself happily to its apparently random disposition, now presumably secure in his understanding of the

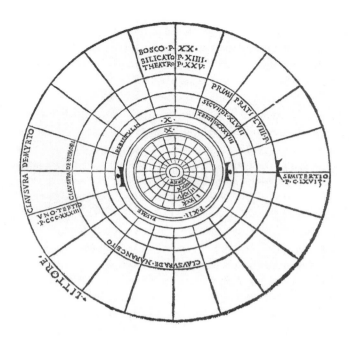

overall site. It is also worth noting that the coherence of the site,
so eloquently articulated in advance of its exploration, is confirmed in part by the straight pathways that lead to its centre;
unlike any route Poliphilo has hitherto taken, these converging
paths lead him down axes along which everything falls into place.

Second, the totality of the garden is remarkable. This takes
various forms, but most obviously its inclusiveness: the complete
collections of herbs, plants, trees, as well as of animals and of
inorganic materials – marbles and semi-precious stones – that
form one of the colonnades; there is even what we would call a
collection of microclimates where each tree is suited to the nature
of the place. A deliberate effort at complete plenitude has always
lurked as a motive behind garden-making; the early botanical
gardens, of course, had just such an ambition and the perfect
circular shape of the Paduan one may even echo the Cytherean

garden here. But, unlike the more functional design of botanical gardens, Colonna's also displays a range of treatments of land: gardens, orchards, meadows, fields. Mountains or first nature, we are told, are absent ('Il quale era loco non di monti devii et desueti'[36]); but the full scale of human invention in the land is otherwise displayed. So to the circularity and theatrical shape of the island and culminating amphitheatre at its centre, we must add the sense of theatre as a conspectus, a complete representation of the world in all its fullness that has been denied to humans since their expulsion from Eden.

Part of the garden's completeness, third, lies in the happy co-operation of verbal and visual languages. What had elsewhere been a frantic research among scattered verbal fragments and visual clues, here is happily whole and coherent, both for Poliphilo himself and for ourselves as readers. The garden is a world of time (narrative) and space (stasis), intellect and senses, physically palpable and yet visionary. If the circular gardens of Cythera are a miniature world, microcosmically constituted as a theatre of memory, then the coincidence of sight with verbal languages only sustains for Poliphilo that fundamental garden experience of rediscovering for the first time what one has known all along.

Fourth, the adjudication between artifice and natural work, at the heart of Poliphilo's as of any garden experience, achieves in Cythera's realm its best opportunity and success. This does not mean that the garden ceases to be anything but contrived and excessively manhandled; the *paragone* of art and nature does not present itself except in full subtlety and ambiguity. The point is that Poliphilo (and as readers we must follow suit) is no longer confused; the competition between *artificalia* and *naturalia*, as in any later cabinet of curiosities, is played out not only with a firm sense of the intricate rules that govern it, but with a proper regard for the likely ambivalence of the outcome. Thus Cythera's fruit trees bear fruit whatever the season; yet the topiary is clipped every day. The natural world is honoured as much as is the artistry of its reformation or reformulation. It is the false impositions of art that are excluded, what the English version calls 'counterfeiting' in the silk garden.[37] That word brings the full rhetorical weight of the Elizabethan criminal offence of making false money to bear upon bad artifice in gardening.

VI

The proper climax of this rare liaison between art and nature, between human culture and physical materials, is the Venus fountain (illus. 30) where Book One of the story ends. A natural source or spring is fashioned into a fountain – a tactful, re-presentation; so too the pergola, the structure of which we might expect to be wood but is the finest gold; this is covered with roses that now, unlike those encountered earlier, are real or natural. The enclosure, like so many medieval representations of a flowery mead, is at once meadow and garden. Away from the pergola, trees flourish in their own naturally perfect forms. The partitions of the enclosure are woven or are graphically rendered as having the zigzag patterns of sliced marble, examples of which may be found on the sanctuary panels of the Byzantine church at Torcello in the Venetian lagoon.

Garden experience in the *Hypnerotomachia* is, as Anthony Littlewood has argued for similar ekphrastic elements in Byzantine romances, an essential part of the tale. I have no space to explore the possible debts of the *Hypnerotomachia* to the various gardens of Byzantine writing, some examples of which would have been conserved and available in manuscript collections in late fifteenth-century Venice and therefore available to a Venetian author. Nor do I think that source-hunting in itself is of much profit in the garden, memory theatre though it may be. But there is a significant melding of narrative and garden experience in the *Hypnerotomachia*, wholly characteristic of Byzantine

romance gardens, when at the end of Book One Polia begins her
story at the fountain of Venus in the circular garden of Cythera.
It is of course in the first instance an apt symbolic location for
such a narrative turn; but more importantly, only when we realize
the full significance of Poliphilo's now completed extension
course in landscape architecture can we grasp the point of a
new beginning in which paradoxically a new ending will be forthcoming. The afterlife of his whole landscape journey and all its
gardens is both retrospective and proleptic.

FOUR

Triggers and Prompts in Landscape Architecture Visitation

I

As Poliphilo discovers, architectural elements, statuary and inscriptions direct his experience of the gardens and landscapes that he encounters (illus. 31). These devices are, by all accounts, of great antiquity in garden-making, but they have continued to be a crucial means by which the consumers of landscape architecture have been drawn into their fullest experience of sites. At least two – buildings and inscriptions – became of exceptional importance during the years of Picturesque gardening for reasons that will shortly be explored, but thereafter they seem to have lost their potency. However, it will be argued that inscriptions at least can continue to play a fundamental role in the ways in which designs are received.

II

The term 'landscape architecture', like the word *fabrique* in French, was originally applied (very logically) to the depiction of buildings in landscape paintings; here the imagery of architectural items would have set the scene or otherwise directed the viewer's attention to some significant event in the painting. From there the French term was borrowed to describe buildings in actual gardens and landscapes, while the English one was drawn into use as a means of describing the relatively new professional work of

31 Poliphilo in a
landscape of ruined
fragments, sculpture
and inscriptions from
the original 1499
Venice edition of the
*Hypnerotomachia
Poliphili.*

designers like Humphry Repton and J. C. Loudon, who usually
but not necessarily inserted architectural work into their landscaping but whose professional provenance was architectural –
'Capability' Brown, for instance, having practised as an architect.
And since these generations of designers were generally thought
to be implementing landscape paintings in real space, it must have
seemed logical to adopt a term from visual art to describe the
new kind of built work. In fact, it was Loudon who invoked the
phrase 'landscape architecture' on the title-page of his 1840
edition of the collected writings of Repton. We may assume that
certain original implications of the phrase clung to its new usage:
if a 'reading' of some architectural element in a landscape painting – whether a Classical temple in one by Claude Lorraine or
Nicolas Poussin or some vernacular building such as a mill or
cottage in Dutch and Flemish paintings – was a means of gaining
some understanding of the visual image (its genre, perhaps, or its
narrative), then a similar habit of response in a real landscape
would clearly draw its visitor into a fuller reception of the signi-

ficance of what lay around him. Especially when landscape designers were consciously invoking pictures as models for their built
work or expecting visitors to recognize pictorial possibilities in
their designs, as they were in various ways throughout the whole
eighteenth century,[1] then the role of architectural insertions would
almost literally help to put the visitor, as we say, in the picture.

Landscape architects, such as William Kent (trained as a
painter himself), would have assumed that buildings could function in paintings as bearers of meaning or at least of expression
(mood), and would have translated that use into their garden
designs. The Temple of Ancient Virtue, for example, that Kent
devised for the Elysian Fields at Stowe was a version of the
Temple of Vesta or (so-called) the Sybil at Tivoli, which Kent
would have undoubtedly seen in person (illus. 32). But visitors to
Stowe are more likely to have seen it represented in innumerable

32 The Temple
of Ancient Virtue
at Stowe,
Buckinghamshire.

33 An engraving of
1746 (J. Wood after
Claude Lorrain) of
a landscape with a
circular temple
modelled on the
Temple of Vesta
(the so-called Sybil's
Temple) at Tivoli.

paintings and engravings, where it spoke variously of Classical
scenes and sacred mysteries appropriate to whatever human
action was depicted in its vicinity (illus. 33). So that we may presume that in the gardens at Stowe, Kent's Temple elicited the
same responses as the identical structure would have provoked
in a painting; it was 'landscape architecture' in the original sense.

The use of a similar circular, columned and domed temple in
many European gardens during the eighteenth and early nineteenth centuries would probably have served a similar purpose
of triggering ideas or sentiments – and this makes an important
further point: namely, Kent may have had one purpose in invoking
the Tivoli building at Stowe that would be different from its use,
say, on the Duncombe Park Terraces in Yorkshire, at Méréville, as
the Monopteros at Kismarton (Eisenstadt) or Charles Cameron's
Temple of Friendship at Pavlovsk. What is important for a
reception study of gardens is not to establish iconographical
meanings inserted or implied by the designer, which in all these

instances may be tied back to a common source, but to track reactions to it by later and less implicated visitors, who often bring to their experiences less focused or less antiquarian knowledge. So at Stowe what would interest a reception study would be the mechanics of response or what we might perhaps call the subtexts of experience, the ways in which a garden visitor saw the Picturesque in action and activated a knowledge or expectation of pictures in a new situation. These more general responses are as interesting as the more focused, modern iconographical analyses that read, say, sacredness into an English context, or identify some strategy whereby the Englishness of the scene was established through some contrast or comparison, satiric or celebratory, with the Classical past.[2] It is not to say, however, that these issues could not be summoned into play by visitors. William Gilpin's *Dialogue* (1748) brings his two visitors to the Temple of Ancient Virtue, where its 'antique' taste and its quartet of 'illustrious' figures from four walks of life prompt a 'noble Panegyric' by one of the speakers on national virtue and responsibility that, though couched in the most general terms, resonates with a mid-eighteenth-century British confidence.[3]

In many ways the theatre was a parallel influence on landscapers' use of architectural items, as the term 'scenery' suggests. Ever since Sebastiano Serlio's codification of the tragic, comic and satiric scenes, audiences could expect stage design to set the scene (as we say) for human actions; it is no accident that at the time when eighteenth-century designers were deploying an increased repertoire of *fabriques* in their gardens, the European theatre was also developing sophisticated settings for the human action in plays – that these were often stereotyped merely underlines their role as indicators to audiences of what they might expect generically in the unfolding dramas.[4]

The differences between history or landscape painting and the theatre on the one hand and the landscape garden on the other are fundamental and bear upon the processes of garden reception.

First, whereas the first two always include actors or depicted personages, garden visitors are both spectator and performer at the same time. Second, whereas the theatre audience is stuck in one place watching scene-changes orchestrated on a single stage before it and the viewer of a painting sees simply one unchanging scene (however skilled the artist is at suggesting spatial depth or temporal passage), garden visitors move easily through a variety of sceneries, with more responsibility for the adjudication of what they encounter, of what ideas and sensations are triggered by those encounters, and of how their experiences are both created or initiated as well as consumed. And the first difference – the double role played out in gardens by their visitors – explains the extraordinary self-consciousness of garden visitation from at least the sixteenth century to the late eighteenth. Not only does such a visitor observe, he or she also 'performs' (discovers a new 'role' in the exploration of spaces); in addition, that double activity is reported in word, image or simply mental reflection.

The pattern books that proliferated during the eighteenth and early nineteenth centuries from Thomas Wright and George-Louis Le Rouge to Gabriel Thouin, J. G. Grohmann and Gijsbert van Laar[5] are often ridiculous in their concoctions of architectural insertions – as bizarre indeed as showrooms of modern garden ornaments. One may legitimately doubt whether these architectural items did much to set a scene, put visitors in a picture or otherwise direct responses to a landscape. They have earned for themselves and for the designs to which they contributed the reputation of curiosities – amusing, eclectic and largely facile gestures by which it was supposed that landscapes would be enhanced or meretriciously decorated. Many were to be contrived in skimpy materials, painted canvas over wooden frames, just like any stage scenery. But what the pattern books do not declare, but probably took for granted, was that all this paraphernalia was proposed in the interests of drawing people somehow into the world of the garden or parkscape.

Some early to mid-eighteenth-century visual material suggests how designs triggered responses in garden visitors. Jacques Rigaud came over from France to draw English scenes in the gardens of Chiswick and Stowe; he had successfully published *Les Promenades de Paris* in 1729, so he was already acutely interested in the activities of visiting, promenading and the exchanges between people and their surroundings. His English scenes depict a density of visitors that is probably an extravagant vision of what a Frenchman thought English society ought to be, as well as a studied compliment to the patrons who commissioned them. Yet – those exaggerations aside – Rigaud's visitors *involve* themselves in the gardens, exploring, examining some item or discussing heaven knows what while promenading (illus. 34). Kent's own sketches of similar gardens, including Chiswick, pick up Rigaud's interest in reception, although more often now the emphasis is on much smaller groups or even individual responses. But if this new gardening was thought of, in Joseph Addison's words, as 'a pretty landskip' (i.e., painting) of a landowner's possessions, then the elements inserted

34 Jacques Rigaud, *The Obelisk at the South-west Entrance to the Gardens at Chiswick House, Middlesex*, c. 1733–4, pen and ink drawing.

into those *landskips* were the three-dimensional equivalent of elements of a picture that led its viewer into a fuller understanding of whatever action was depicted.

It is difficult to know at some specific designed sites what that action would have been. Clearly, a ruined Gothic building in an English garden would have promoted a different scenario than exactly the same kind of insertion or 'found object' at, say, the Désert de Retz in France or the Villa Pallavicini outside Genoa. A small ruined abbey for William Shenstone at The Leasowes or the extensive ruins of Fountains Abbey purchased by William Aislabie as a termination point for his gardens at Studley Royal encouraged thoughts for an Englishman of Protestant traditions that derived from the sixteenth-century dissolution of the monasteries. Yet these would have been entirely different from the reaction of the Genoese who were probably being encouraged to recall Tasso or Ariosto while visiting Pallavicini, or indeed from a Roman Catholic landowner like Philip Southcote when he gazed at the chapel on St Anne's Hill near his farm at Woburn in Surrey. The point is that the role of buildings – whether genuine ruins or fabrications – was to suggest a train of thought or some 'action' appropriate to the visitors who were involving themselves in these sites.

Some texts help us to follow these experiences. Pope's gardener, after his death, published a description of the famous Twickenham grotto; it consisted of lists of the geological specimens inserted into the walls along with their provenance, both geographical and personal (who gave it to Pope and from where it came). This argues strongly for John Searle's use of a published text to formalize the strategy of visitation that Pope himself encouraged or conducted, with the grotto visitor knowing or learning by enquiry what any one element was. Similarly, when the gardener at Rousham, John Macclary, tried to tempt the absentee owners to return and enjoy its enchantments, he stolidly took them through a narrative where the buildings, statues and prospects all trigger some response. This suggests that even a visitation by those who might be expected to know the site well (because they own it) consists of inserting oneself into the narrative, meaning or 'action' of the place as both player and spectator; Macclary is rehearsing them in what he thinks would be their responses.

There are both losses and gains in transferring 'landscape architecture' from painting or stage to a real topography. One potential loss is the uncertainty as to what role the visitor must play, given the absence of any explicit scenario provided by a theatre script or pictorial subject matter. It is that lacuna that some guidebooks supplied by drawing out of the architectural and other insertions a series of narrative moments or episodes, although this could also be driven by the alertness, knowledge and responsiveness of the visitor.

A literary example, unconnected with a real site, occurs in Joseph Spence's *Polymetis* (1747). This was essentially a guide to the many Roman gods and goddesses, their nomenclature and attributes; the book went through several editions (1755, 1774) including a school version (1764) that had six editions of its own, thereby confirming its author's sense that his contemporaries needed to be reminded of their mythological inheritance. What concerns us is that Spence proposes to lay out this memory theatre in a landscape 'rather wild than regular' through which are scattered a series of temples, each containing a whole icono-graphical arsenal pertaining to the relevant deity. The eponymous Polymetis conducts his readers around this landscape and draws from its landscape architecture the lessons and facts that he thinks it important to remember:

You see that Rotunda, with a Colonnade running round it, on the brow of the hill? Within that, are the great celestial deities: as the milder ones relating to the human mind and civil life, (Fidelity, Clemency; Peace, Concord; Plenty, Health; all the

Mental or Moral Deities, of the better sort) are placed in the Colonnade about it. . . . That temple, lower down the hill to the right, contains the beings which preside over the element of fire . . . You may call this, if you please, the temple of the Sun and Stars . . .That Octagon, opposite to it on the left, is the Temple of the Winds, and of the imaginary beings of the air. Those two temples on either hand below them contain, one the deities of the Waters, and the other the deities of the Earth . . .

The statues are placed in niches made for them, and ornamented with copies of such ancient relievos or pictures as relate to them. In their pedestals, I have contrived drawers, to put in the medals, gems, prints and drawings . . .[6]

While over-determined in the precision of its references and, further, more concerned with the accumulation and communication of Classical lore than with how these events might contribute to the landscape, Spence's examples do suggest clearly how he at least – a Professor of both Poetry and Modern History at Oxford – envisaged visitors responding to a landscape with Classical insertions.

Yet in large landscape spaces visitors could be distracted by irrelevancies that the artistry of painter or theatre director and actor had eliminated or at least subdued. Gilpin's Stowe *Dialogue* is again instructive here: after confronting the Temple of Ancient Virtue, the two visitors learn what next to focus their attention on and tease out the significance of an adjacent building – the ruined Temple of Modern Virtue ('I suppose . . . intended to contrast with this new Building'). One visitor even remarks on the happiness of having a companion who can help him isolate, 'moralize' upon and connect the garden's different elements.

But what is potentially a loss in translating the experience of a painting to experience in a garden gains the compensation of giving to the garden visitors the liberty to organize, respond, even perhaps invent, the 'action' in which they participate. And in gardens without any or many *fabriques* – as was urged by one particular vogue among early nineteenth-century landscapers – the visitor invented or free-associated, yet in ways learnt in the first instance from a landscape of triggers and prompts. This enlarged freedom of responsiveness can be addressed if we compare Thomas Whately's *Observations on Modern Gardening* (1770), when he discusses the issue of buildings in the landscape, with Joseph Heely's similar discussion in his *Letters on the Beauties of Hagley, Envill and the Leasowes* (1777).[7] Whately argues that since garden buildings have ceased to be useful as habitations, they are now 'considered as objects only'. As such, it is their exterior treatment and their siting that direct experience and responses; they focus the character, idea or meaning of a particular scene – 'they are so observable, so obvious at a glance, so easily retained in the memory, they mark the spots where they are placed with so much strength'. Heely, no doubt because he was describing three gardens where the incidence of architectural elements was less insistent than at some of the sites Whately discussed, is more apt to stress the train of thought that some item would provoke and, further, gives as much attention to the formal qualities of natural features, which nevertheless function as prompts in exactly the way that architecture could do. When Heely gazes down the glen at Hagley, he takes in a

> variety of trees, beeches, oaks, ashes, in the utmost confusion; some tottering with age, intermingling their naked roots; others thin and tall, aslant or straight, mix, crowd, and entwine their luxuriant branches; among which, several rills are taught to dribble their mazy course, in natural worn passages, down the shelving banks . . .

It would appear a wholly natural scene, except that 'taught' recalls the reader, as the contrivance of the scene would the actual visitor,

to its design, at the same time alerting both reader and potential
visitor to the necessity and excitements of response. For Heely,
indeed, such recognitions are as much an element of reception
as of design intention; his *Letters* mark an interesting advance in
explicating the former rather than eliciting design precepts.

III

If the Picturesque has a bad press these days, understandably
given its inert invocation as a journalistic term implying 'attractive' or 'pleasing to look at', maybe even 'quaint', then a more
nuanced understanding of how the original Picturesque used
prompts and triggers will not only enhance its historical reputation but instruct us also in how landscape designs might work
upon those who explore them. Architectural items, as well as
sculpture, are a means of introducing people to unfamiliar,
perhaps even uncongenial sites by getting them to view these
locations in terms of familiar patterns of behaviour; after all,
we all tend to respond to new encounters by relying on what we
already know or like. In the eighteenth century that meant asking
people to envisage wild, forbidding, uncultivated or even just
plain unadorned land as if it were the subject-matter of admired
and familiar or even imaginary paintings. Especially when the
'new' and 'English' landscaping was replacing the elaborately
detailed and structured Baroque garden, some means was called
for that made the sparser and apparently less artful designs
appealing: if you were no longer negotiating terraces, reviewing
manicured hedges, embroidered parterres or clusters of sculpture, ducking into grottoes or admiring the upward swish of
fountains (all the familiar apparatus of late seventeenth-century
European garden art), then to be initiated into this new world
where what now mattered were sweeping lawns, clumps of trees,
irregular bodies or falls of water, meandering paths and glimpses

outwards into countryside beyond the garden, reassuring appeals to established and familiar elements of landscape paintings were particularly acceptable.

Besides architectural items, inscriptions could play a similar role in recalling what one already knew and in mediating the new experience in the midst of which one now found oneself. The role of inscriptions in landscape architecture has a different history from that of architectural items and posed different challenges to visitors, although their use shares the same impulse to pull visitors into the experience of place. Yet it must be confessed that professional colleagues who practise landscape architecture today often forcibly express the view that words are not a part of their vocabulary, indeed are somehow to be avoided as being literary or intellectual; this presumably derives in its turn from a widespread twentieth-century view that the arts should be kept separate, each medium relying on its own unique qualities;[8] landscape architecture being – in this view – visual, can have no truck with the verbal. This of course flies in the face of garden history since at least the Romans, for inscriptions have played a variety of roles in landscape design and experience; more generally, architecture and writing have been ineluctably linked (Vitruvius could be our guide there[9]). That this is not a lost art is clear from the work of one contemporary figure in modern landscape architecture, Ian Hamilton Finlay, who has significantly extended or at least revived our understanding of what gardens can do, an achievement that is realized in great part via the use of inscriptions. And since one of his 'More Detached Sentences on Gardening in the Manner of Shenstone' of 1982 asserts that 'The inscription seems out of place in the modern garden. It jars on our secularism . . .',[10] he also identifies a central issue that this chapter needs to confront.

IV

Michel Foucault has written of 'study, analysis, description and "reading" (as some like to say nowadays)'[11] – and he puts reading into inverted commas. But the 'reading' of (or in) gardens is not a modern development, or, as he implies, a neologism. To stay within Foucault's own culture, the Abbé Delille's poem on *Les Jardins*, first published in 1782, is endlessly concerned with how the physical experience of a garden can elicit from its visitors a range of feelings, ideas, images – and words;[12] indeed, this was by no means an unfamiliar perspective at the time – Claude-Henri Watelet in France and C.C.L. Hirschfeld in Germany also understood garden experience in that way. Delille says that gardens address visitors' feelings and memories with a 'voix secrète' (1.17) as well as an affective eye. If garden visitors see pictures ('Un jardin à mes yeux est un vaste tableau'/ 'A garden in my eyes is a vast painting' [1.11]), these pictures stimulate the mind to recall stories that require verbal articulation; so that they may, for instance, hear Petrarch talking to Laura, since 'Tout parle, tout émeut' (everything speaks, everything emits) in these poetic gardens (IV.102). The garden-maker is therefore advised to learn not only from such famous painters as Nicolaes Berghem or Nicolas Poussin but equally from poets like Homer and Virgil. And, as Giulia Pacini has shrewdly noted,[13] it is the digressions of poets that may best serve Delille's gardenist – 'Si leur muse en marchant se permet quelque écart,/ Ce détour me rit plus que le chemin lui-même' (If their muse permits itself to turn aside while walking, this detour amuses me more than the path itself) (IV.87) – and as a result of this literary model a series of episodes may be introduced along the garden path, episodes that have the potential of verbal narrativity.

Delille then suggests some possible mechanisms by which to enable these 'episodes'– the most obvious of which being the inscription, a set of engraved words like 'A nos braves marins

35 Engraving of the
Monument to Captain
Cook at Méréville,
from Alexandre de
Laborde, *Descriptions
des nouveaux jardins de
la France et de ses anciens
châteaux* (Paris, 1808).

mourants pour la patrie' (To our brave sailors lost for their country) (IV.98). It was in fact similar lines commemorating Captain
Cook from Delille's poem that were inscribed on the monument
dedicated to that explorer by the Marquis de Laborde at Méréville
in 1788 and designed by Hubert Robert (illus. 35). Since the poem
went through nine editions in its first year, its diffusion was
considerable enough that by the time four lines were adapted
from it for the monument at Méréville they could easily have

brought to the mind of educated visitors at Méréville Delille's lengthier, published panygeric of Cook and the story that it recited. A similar repertoire of verses, fragments to prompt recollection of sustained passages, was used by Girardin at Ermenonville, like the altar dedicated 'A la reverie'. Watelet's *Essai sur les jardins* seems to provide similar prompts by the expedient of invented rather than actual quotations, which he gives his readers towards the end of his small book.[14] That is to say, we have not discovered any authors for the quatrains that he cites (he may have composed them himself) and can only assume that they were indeed, as he implies, inscribed in his garden of Moulin Joli; if they were not inscribed (whether or not they were invented or actual quotations), then they are doubly imaginary, being adduced in the literary text to help his reader understand the experience of a garden site where the sensitive soul is prompted to bring into play literary sentiments and ideas.

This promotion of response can also go beyond the mechanism of actual inscriptions. Both Watelet and especially Delille suggest that visitors may be prompted by the careful contrivances of landscape architectural formal design, not just the architectural insertions already discussed, but items like a spring or a stream, to recall similar effects from 'nos vieux romans, ou la fable, ou l'histoire' (our old novels, or fable, or history) (III.78). It is clear that the French Picturesque garden shares a basic strategy of the Picturesque elsewhere: to unite the pen and the pencil (the word with the image[15]) so that words are invoked to enlarge and enhance the full visual and sensual appeal of a garden for its visitors.

V

We could and indeed must go further back to trace this double regard – verbal and visual – in both human treaties with the world in general and our experience in gardens. Indeed, in her stimulating book *Vitruvius: Writing the Body of Architecture*, Indra Kagis McEwen traces the intimate allegiances between word and design in Roman architectural writing (which, in the absence of any early writings on landscape architecture, will be the closest to our topic). She reminds us that Vitruvius thought that the architect must be trained in nine disciplines, of which writing is the first and foremost;[16] writing is essential because it empowers the memory, the memory of past deeds and events (including buildings) as well as the memories we have ourselves and bring to built work. But Vitruvius also argues that architects are more than mere craftsmen inasmuch as they rely on discussion and writing (p. 33), which enhances and authorizes their professional discipline.

In Roman landscape architectural practice we can also glimpse the authority of writing in association with practice in various ways. Cicero owned villas called after the literary genres of Tragedy and Comedy; he also emphasized the power of place and so of the memories that it would engender, for the articulation of which there were always words. At Pliny's Tuscan villa there were names inscribed in the plants and topiary work – local affirmations of master and gardener – as well as evident recollections of Roman landscape paintings. What emerges of Horace's villa from hints in his poetry is a cluster of associations, ideas and memories;[17] that is, of course, endemic to the literary medium, but the implication – supported by many other hints in the Roman discussion of gardens – is that the haptic experience of gardens was not considered sufficient without associated ideas and memories, for which the verbal – uttered aloud or mentally – was the vital medium. The Renaissance, too, made many of its gardens of such elaborate forms and images that the educated visitor at least found the need to put words to physical forms; one has to imagine, in fact, that the visitation of gardens like the Villa Lante at Bagnaia and the Villa d'Este involved a kind of peripatetic *ekphrasis*, whereby the visitor translated into some form of verbal meditation or commentary the experiences that came to him through all his senses as he walked the sites.

However we choose to explain and narrate the continuity between Renaissance garden art and the later Picturesque or Romantic garden experience, I believe the latter holds a special place in the European history of inscriptions in gardens: special, because the late eighteenth-century witnesses a critical watershed in garden design where the complicity of words or texts with gardens was brought into question for the first time (as far as I know). On one side the divide was a plethora of verbal injunctions to the visitor located in a garden, or at least visual prompts demanding verbal 'translation'; this is nothing other than a Renaissance tradition writ large and sentimental in early Romanticism. On the other side of the divide was the notion that the sensitive visitor needed none of these items to stimulate his or her imagination and emotions in a designed (or indeed even un-designed) landscape, that explicit prompts or 'emblems' frustrated the free range of the individual imagination within the landscape. However, what these divergent views nevertheless had in common was the agreed need to promote a visitor's response, which became an inevitable or necessary part of garden and landscape experience; they diverged simply but importantly in the ways by which they thought it could be achieved, with long-term consequences whichever route was chosen.

This radical duality as to how a garden visitor might behave or be prompted to behave was mirrored in design philosophy and its treatises, where the promotion of *fabriques* and inscriptions was favoured by one group, their suppression in favour of the individual's intuition of the apparently unmediated expressions of nature herself by another. Gabriel Thouin is summarizing this same distinction when he remarks in the preface to *Plans raisonnés de toutes les espèces de jardins* (1820) that there were basically two garden modes, what could be called 'mannerist' and 'natural'.

VI

Among the crucial long-term consequences of this late eighteenth-century watershed, as I've called it, is the current professional retreat from, or dislike of, verbal supplements in landscape architecture, anything in short that directs the visitor's attention away into realms that are vaguely gestured to as 'literary'. A lively but inconclusive debate has been waged for some time now in North America on the desirability or possibility of 'meaning' in landscape architecture, with meaning always seeming to be couched in discursive (i.e., verbal) not figurative or visual terms. Even the most articulate and verbally driven commentators – Marc Treib, Laurie Olin, Bob Riley (all designers, by the way) – are doubtful whether designed landscapes can 'mean' and / or that such meanings are translatable into words.[18] A brief example of this stance might be the remarks (in this case) of an architectural historian, Richard Guy Wilson, about the Mall in Washington, DC:

> The Mall is a powerful symbol, and as all great symbols it is ambiguous in interpretation and meaning. And it is physical, visual, and spatial. Historians try to reduce all experience to words, but in the end words cannot adequately represent the passions, the beliefs, and the experience of the Mall. In spite of the battles or showdowns by politicians, protectors, users and architects, the Mall escapes exact definition. Great symbols defy exactness: the Mall succeeds and endures.[19]

This is, incidentally, a familiar, quasi-logical manoeuvre among designers as well as some commentators – ambiguity in interpretation and the chance (or is it the danger?) of contested meanings provoke and justify a retreat from the need for their articulation or even their presence. It also has, it must be admitted, some historical justification: we can locate the beginnings of this mistrust of verbalizing at a time, towards the later eighteenth century, of the breakdown of public, social and generalized understandings of art, which John Barrell has examined;[20] when the public role of arts was questioned, when there could be no guarantee of any commonly shared response, when the rule of every person having their own opinion (*tot homines, quot sententiae*) prevailed, it may have seemed more plausible or even practical to refrain from translating your reactions into words or at least to keep them to yourself.

But, to my mind, there is a far more interesting question than 'can gardens mean?'– which in fact should be construed more as a question of reception, how the construction of meanings is achieved by successive visitors, than whether designers implant meanings on their sites.[21] A more fruitful path of enquiry is to ask what has become these days of that branch of Picturesque theory and practice that strongly endorsed words in the garden and / or verbal supplements to visual prompts. The alternative route – Thouin's 'natural' way – is well travelled by practitioners and their critics – from 'Capability' Brown and Jean-Marie Morel, with their apparently artless landscapes and embrace of natural processes, to their countless if assorted modern successors, who favour either a wordless horticultural fecundity, even if technologically sustained by the greenhouse, or who, as with ecological purists, see the integrity of their plant palette as the only feasible 'meaning' to be entertained.[22] No, that strain or tradition or line of landscape architecture is secure, strong and well documented and rehearsed. In contrast, what I have called Thouin's 'mannerist' route – though an unhappy and pejorative label that many will still unfortunately think only too appropriate – is unexplored and uncelebrated.

VII

This route has many more destinations than one might imagine: large-scale inscriptions by Jacques Simon in the agricultural fields of France or Dieter Kienast, invoking ET IN ARCADIA EGO as the

railing along a private woodland belvedere in the Swiss country-side near Zürich (illus. 36), are examples that come to mind;[23] so do elements of Battery Park City like the railings in front of the Winter Gardens, recently restored after 9 / 11, with their quotations from famous writers on New York City, or the FDR Memorial by Lawrence Halprin in Washington, DC, where the site is replete with quotations from FDR's famous fireside talks on the radio to which reference is explicitly made elsewhere at the Memorial (illus. 37).

But the crucial example that springs to mind is Ian Hamilton Finlay, for his pursuit of cultural agendas that rely upon both the expedient of inscriptions and the verbal elaborations that may be expected of other visual and horticultural items. A very recent and not yet completed project (it lacked the proposed planting when I saw and photographed it in February 2003) is in the grounds of St Michael's, Brandon Hill, in Bristol. The site (illus. 38) contains a fine Georgian church now used as a concert hall; its grounds, the former churchyard, slope steeply from a road that runs across the back of the church site down to the famous George Street, from which steps lead up to the main entrance of

37 Visitors at the FDR Memorial, Washington, DC, designed by Lawrence Halprin.

38 The churchyard of St Michael's, Brandon Hill, Bristol, with some of the installations by Ian Hamilton Finlay.

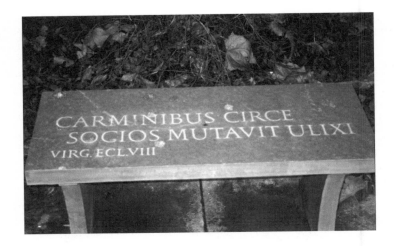

39 Inscription on a bench in the grounds of St Michael's Church, Bristol.

the church. The commission to Finlay produced three pairs of benches in different parts of these grounds, an oval medallion laid in the ground of the rear car park, a wall-plaque and an inscribed post of teak; all but the post are in Caithness stone (illus. 39). On all of these items are inscribed quotations from Virgil, Ovid and the composer Janáček, referring in some way to the transformative power of music. One of Janáček's remarks, taken from his letters, inscribed on a plaque affixed to the wall of the church itself, also alludes to the natural life of trees and the longevity that the composer associates with his carving into their trunks of words that otherwise were dissipated in the air, like sung notes:

> On the path I'd plant oaks which would endure for centuries
> And into their trunks I'd carve the words I shouted in the air.

From Virgil are taken lines that profess how music draws down the moon from heaven ('Carmina vel aeolo possunt deducere lunam'), or how Circe's songs transform Odysseus' men (both from *Eclogue* VIII). Words, alluding to Ovid's *Metamorphoses*, revolve around the edge of the circular medallion, as GIRL INTO REED: REED INTO AIR: AIR INTO MUSIC, and by implication as the engraved circle continues for a second cycle MUSIC INTO GIRL, and so on. On benches in the Memorial Garden is another pair of lines from Janáček where he confesses to consumption by a heat that cannot catch fire, 'Like a heavy beautiful dream in which I am bewitched', by which we may infer his passionate absorption by music.

Now these words, calling one to leave the pathways that skirt the church building and sit or read in the adjacent spaces, might also recall us to the endless connections between music and nature, between words and music, between words and places like this, in fact to the very theme of connections and transformations themselves – the unison that words on the teak post proclaim: 'when you and I speak together' (*Hoc mihi conloquium tecum manebit*). But it must quickly be asked how it is that Latin can speak at all to visitors here today. There is a chorus of answers, not all by any means singing in unison. One says that unfamiliar Latin simply evokes a strangeness, an otherness, analogous perhaps to the alternative world we inhabit in and with music, which abides no verbal translation. Another argues that Latin might delay our full understanding – that comprehension arguably requires a more sustained interrogation, at least until we obtain a crib sheet supplied in the church / concert hall office. Yet another would say that Latin secures an elite and very select group of readers, who can respond as privileged auditors to an old, 'dead' and largely pastoral tongue. However, the presence of Janáček prevents too easy a dismissal of these 'dead' languages, for, after all, if he also speaks to us and in English (albeit presumably a translation), these inscriptions are not necessarily just an arcane ritual. However, it must be admitted that Finlay's use of Latin in his projects – perhaps we might also have, these days, to include any language other than English – distances and self-selects the audience for his garden inscriptions.

But whether in Latin or the vernacular tongue of Bristol, it is equally clear that inscriptions are a predictable item that one might expect in an urban as in a country churchyard; the elegy by Thomas Gray is a cultural commonplace, and nearby in the Bristol City Art Gallery is a contemporary painting by David Inshaw of just such a country churchyard and its solitary figure amidst the gravestones, with its very verbal title, *Our Days Were a Joy and Our Paths Through Flowers*.[24] So the churchyard site of St Michael's does make Finlay's inscriptions plausible, while at the same time reminding us that the new use of a Georgian church as a concert hall for chamber music also makes yet another metamorphosis or transformation necessary in the surrounding garden. Benches, walls, inlaid plaques and inscriptions are familiar items in a garden-cum-graveyard – perhaps only the austere and upright teak shaft is more of a curiosity; so we are able to inhabit the garden and meditate as best we can or wish on the connections between worship, music, metamorphoses and the natural world (of trees especially, for the column is wooden after all). Even if we don't connect all the dots, the garden has been made into something special by the supplements invented for it.

It is said that the Emperor Augustus, under whom Ovid and Virgil composed their poems, always wrote down things that were important; he even wrote rather than spoke when he had important things to communicate to his wife, Livia.[25] In this modern age of mechanical reproduction, writing something down, especially when the medium is stone, teak, granite or marble, still lends them more than usual importance. If words are 'articulate thought',[26] written words are emphatically articulate. We look and attend, perhaps more so when the place where we find writing does not automatically suggest itself as a locus of communication. Indeed, the old rhetorical device or mode of *prosopopeia* was invented to designate the special situation in which a poet calls upon an absent voice to speak to the privileged visitor at a given spot – that voice may be of the *genius loci* itself

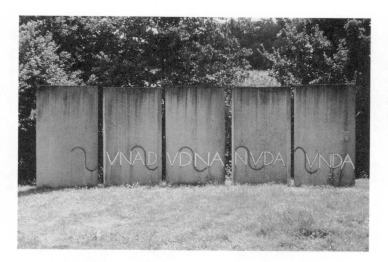

40 *UNDA/WAVE*, designed by Ian Hamilton Finlay with Ron Costley, concrete and stainless steel, 1976, Max-Planck Institute, Stuttgart (photographed before 1985).

or of a former inhabitant. Words establish or reaffirm the meaning and nature of place.

This is evident in Finlay's contributions to the headquarters of the German research institute, the Max-Planck, outside Stuttgart.[27] As we descend the slope below the main building of this physical sciences research centre, we encounter a set of five curved concrete panels (illus. 40) on four of which are inscribed a repeated word; as we read from left to right these letters gradually resolve themselves into UNDA, the Latin for wave (from which root we derive undulations). Should we fail to decipher it, the panels themselves and the wavy line wrapped around each of the words (the conventional printer / compositor's sign for 'transpose' or switch around) prompt us further; a wave runs through, overrides and finally composes the Latin itself. The panels maybe recall the hanging concrete screens on the roof of the main building we have just left, and the line of corrected UNDAS leads our eye and feet to another pair of upright panels poised over a pool of water in which the reversed German word for ship reveals itself, *Schiff*. Occasionally the breeze may

41 Pond and inscribed plinth, designed by Ian Hamilton Finlay with Ron Costley, 1976, Max-Planck Institute, Stuttgart (photographed before 1985).

ruffle the surface of this small pool (we might recall another inscription, *Windflower*, wrought in iron and placed in the flower-beds by the main building), and by implication the two upright panels of the *Schiff* become sails in the wind. We learn something, this suggests, through reflection! Further down the valley is a pond, where a boardwalk leads us to a pedestal that rises out of the reeds (illus. 41): on its sloping surface it proclaims, in a formulation that Finlay is evidently fond of and invokes elsewhere, HIC JACET PARVULUM QUONDDAM EX ACQUA LONGIORE EXCERPTUM ('Here lies a small water excerpted from a larger [one]'). The graphic parody of an ancient inscription – its weathered lettering, the Roman vs for Us (not transcribed here) – combined with the *Hic jacet* . . . ('Here lies . . . ') of graveyard Latin makes this moment seem like a voice from the distant past, a message from the depths of the pond.

Waves, geological undulations (the German *wellenformig*), water, wind and the examination of the structure of the whole natural world from experimental, small excerpted specimens are all the business of physics research, so that Finlay has in one sense simply drawn out the implications of the place where we find ourselves and writ the *genius loci* large in word and image within the parkland of the Max-Planck Institute. Again, as at Bristol, we have the challenge of interpretation, except that the UNDA panels and the German *Schiff* speak more directly in this place, and only the dead language of HIC JACET may defy instant reading.

There is the element of crossword-solving, of conundrum and riddle about these scattered inscriptions of Finlay's; his words tease us, if we wish, into solving their elliptical clues or accepting that something is unknown, beyond us here.[28] This is not, I would suggest, such an oddity in a garden, where mystery, occluded meanings and a concentration of experience need to be unpacked: from the earliest modern gardens of *Hypnerotomachia Poliphi* or *Le Roman de la rose* to the gardens of Julie's 'Elysium' in Rousseau's *La nouvelle Héloïse* or Proust's *Jean Santeuil*, visitors had to puzzle out the meanings and implications of where they were and what they encountered; even the adjudication of whether a scene is natural or cultural, as in Rousseau's novel, contributes to the unravelling of what is not immediately transparent.[29] So we might argue that words in Finlay's installations – as perhaps in other and earlier sites – help us through their own verbal challenges to re-engage with the mysterious and arcane elements of garden worlds when so much else in our modern surroundings seems wearily familiar.

VIII

The issue of how available are inscriptions in Latin or cultural references to the classics comes to the fore in a public park, such as Finlay's Stockwood Park at Luton, completed in 1991 (Stuttgart is something of a compromise, being a private institution whose grounds are open to the public). Stephen Bann, in his careful, interpretative essay on Stockwood Park entitled 'A Luton Arcadia',[30] touches on the comprehensibility of Finlay's work in this truly public park, but leaves it unresolved. In Finlay's own private demesne of Little Sparta visitors may – probably must – accept that its frequent recourse to inscriptions constitutes a personal language of artistic faith, clearly urgent and crucial to the garden's creator, and that the accessibility of the 'messages' will depend upon what skills, knowledge, imaginative and interpretative invention and information (about Finlay's career specifically) a visitor brings to the visit. Indeed, there is, for those who need it, a corpus of essays – including a book-length *primer*[31] – that can instruct the interested and curious. On the other hand, it is also arguable that Little Sparta offers much to those who simply explore its richly established glades and pathways and are struck, as who in fact cannot be, by the intricate series of insertions. Visitors, when admitted to Little Sparta, are indeed left by Finlay to their own devices and to explore on their own. The striking incidence of inscriptions throughout the garden will amuse, perplex, provoke or speak to visitors depending on what they

42 *Flock* in
Stockwood Park,
Luton, Bedfordshire,
designed by Ian
Hamilton Finlay
with Bob Burgoyne,
completed in 1991.

bring to their visit, out of which different processes may emerge
the beginnings of a larger comprehension. But in the final resort
it is a site that through the activity of the poet-gardener himself
speaks to the privileged visitor – *prosopopeia*, again. List who may.

Luton is by its very nature open to everybody and generally
does not partake of the enclosed mystery that hangs over many
gardens; above all it cannot propose its imagery and inscriptions
as the personal utterances of a proprietor. Although one of
them reads 'I SING FOR THE MUSES AND MYSELF', visitors cannot
assume that this is Finlay speaking – and indeed they would be
right, for it is not Finlay but the Emperor Julian and others
before him who address us at that moment. Indeed, we are
reminded sharply that this is public space when we approach
Stockwood Park through a former private enclave, an adjacent
eighteenth- / nineteenth-century walled garden, then come face
to face with a blank hedge and with one of William Kent's vases
originally created for Alexander Pope's garden at Twickenham in
the 1720s. Only then do we emerge into the more predictable
open spaces of public parkland that extend into a golf course

beyond (illus. 42). In more ways than one this is a very different world from Little Sparta.

The park aroused little warmth or comprehension among local inhabitants when it was opened to the public, a reception that I noticed myself during my only visit and was invited to explain to an out-of-work father hauling his kid in a pushchair what the MUSES tree plaque was all about. To be fair, the park itself makes no claim to easy comprehension, on the contrary: another inscription on a woodland herm plays with anagrams of APHRODITE, of which the first is 'I HARD POET', while the curved brick exedra, the most conspicuous architectural insertion in the park, is concerned apparently to correct some Classical errors by substituting modern words. Yet these 'ERRATA OF OVID' (illus. 43), as they are called, may, along with the nearby tree columns, be the easiest clue to what is going on here if we give them even a moment's calm attention. The double tree column says BETULA PENDULA in the language of the Swedish botanist Linnaeus and then SILVER BIRCH in our vernacular. The series of Ovidian *errata* that run along the wall transpose DAPHNE into LAUREL, but also NARCISSUS into NARCISSUS. It is surely no hard poetry to read here how the Classical worlds of myth and botanical nomenclature need sometimes to be translated, metamorphosed, for contemporary consumption, while on other occasions we can marvel that their currency is still ours.

Perhaps visitors might go further and put their own words to the one non-verbal item in the park, a half-buried chunk of Classical masonry: this is no less than (a) 'buried capital', the cultural resources of which we might exhume. Or, again, on one of the blocks of stone in the meadow (see illus. 42), on which mothers perch while their children play nearby, is inscribed the dictionary definition of a FLOCK, so that we can assume, wrily, that these lumps of stone are a modern version of sheep that once might have been pastured here. So visitors might translate the Classical world of shepherds – Theocritan eclogue or Claudean

pastoral – into its only feasible and plausible modern form: another necessary *erratum*.

Stephen Bann calls Finlay's work at Luton 'a mature statement of belief', which is fine if you are already acquainted with Finlay's convictions about the artist's role in changing the world, into which world his various strategies of action must necessarily be carried. Gardens, even public gardens, are attacks not retreats (one of Finlay's wonderful aphorisms), and what is 'attacked' at Luton is a matrix of contemporary phenomena that are obviously more palpable, more insistent than they are within Finlay's own realm of Little Sparta (illus. 44). What Finlay's project does is to confront the 'secularization of culture' in a place like Stockwood Park and erase it (an *erratum*) by substituting fresh formulations of magical, sacred imagery. Words, which in the days when Finlay was working largely in concrete poetry he

43 A detail of the Ovid's Errata wall in Stockwood Park, Luton, designed by Ian Hamilton Finlay with Bob Burgoyne, 1991.

called 'a model of order . . . set in a space full of doubt',[32] offer intimations of an order that may not be fully understood until the space of doubts is first acknowledged; but the words hint at the scope of those eventual recoveries. At Luton the bland, empty provisions of contemporary landscape architecture are confronted with a counter discourse; the expected monovocal and monovisual aspects of public landscaping are met with a discursive complexity more usually found in private gardens. The empty space of contemporary life at its more depressing and drained is thus transformed into a stage where visitors are required to re-construct themselves as historically attuned searchers after more than surface matters.

IX

The burden of these garden 'attacks' is borne at Luton by verbal inscriptions, which further delay the reception of Finlay's various meanings for folk who generally expect the instant elucidation of advertisement or TV captions. While this particular project is absorbing and important in itself, on this occasion it suggests an agenda of larger issues that involve the reception of built work. Finlay uses words, as we have noted earlier garden-makers did, to signal to his visitors the wide range of political, cultural and intellectual ideas and impulses that inform gardens. His words do not initiate narratives; in this he recalls Delille's interest in episodes, isolated ideas and concepts; indeed, one of Finlay's own aphorisms – '(Classical) landscape, n. a stand of concepts'[33] – insists. The ubiquitous HIC JACET, to be found again at Little Sparta, recalls us to the necessary concept that a garden is a small, concentrated set of extracts from a larger, less ordered world.

Landscape architects are loath to admit how wide a range of reference is endemic to their work; as a result they seem often to have lost control of their full professional territory to planners,

engineers, horticulturalists, each of whom has a much more limited agenda (pragmatic, readily achievable and unstrenuously available). It is in fact difficult, even for landscape architects themselves it seems, to persuade people that their best work involves – because they draw upon – a whole nexus of human concerns and activities: these include ideas of the physical world (nature), philosophy and metaphysics, politics and economics, notions of sacred or privileged spaces, social customs and rituals, and play, performance and fantasy. Within this cluster of human resources, words are central to their articulation and understanding, as Vitruvius long ago realized. Finlay may recall us, then, to the 'mannerist' line of descent from later eighteenth-century gardens, that watershed of modernity. It is a reminder that gardens played and must continue to play fundamental roles in political and cultural life, that they offered worlds where even forms of

44 'See Poussin/Hear Lorrain': an elegiac inscription in Ian Hamilton Finlay's own garden of Little Sparta, Scotland, made with John Andrew, 1975.

secularism were treated with profound and moving energy and more often than not reaffirmed sacred issues – of sublimity, for example. Texts in gardens, like buildings, have perhaps always been dialectical, confrontational, simply because they do not partake of the botanical materials that otherwise make up that site and are what people now expect gardens or landscapes to be: in an age when – as Finlay says – inscriptions seem wholly inappropriate, words are even more likely to affront us. Today the *text*ured garden can also confront and challenge the bland routines of our usual place-making; its triggers and prompts can alert us to some hidden resources in ourselves and our cultures.

FIVE

Verbal versus Visual Responses in Garden Visitation

Perhaps you will ask me, 'Why all this long description? Should not
I rather have drawn plans of this magnificent place . . . ?'
JEAN-DENIS ATTIRET[1]

Fabriques and inscriptions were a means of drawing visitors into
a fuller experience of gardens. But this experience itself was more
complete and satisfactory for many if it could be articulated, spelt
out verbally or represented visually. Visitors sketched in gardens
(nowadays they would also take photographs), wrote memoranda
or made entries in their journals; they talked and exchanged
impressions with their companions as they strolled or discussed
their reactions after the visit; they delved into some available
guidebook to find out how to respond (perhaps to confirm their
own intuitions about what they were seeing), or they maybe
bought engravings (these days it would be postcards) to fix the
visit more securely in their memories. All of the above are prime
materials for a reception study of landscape architecture, which
may prove to be interestingly different from a narrative of
design. Further, the alternative opportunities of words and
images in which to recount their experiences clearly concerned
many visitors, so that we need also to investigate the different
resources for a study of gardens that come with verbal or visual
accounts of reception.

I

A visitor in April 1457 to the garden of the Palazzo Medici in
Florence gives some hints as to how it was designed and laid out,
but just as crucially he tries to explain his reactions. The letter
is from Niccolò de' Carissimi to Francesco Sforza, Duke of
Milan:[2]

> A garden done in the finest of polished marbles with divers
> plants, which seems a thing not natural but painted. And
> among other things there is an adder in the form of the
> device of Your Excellency, and beside it there is the shield
> with the arms of the aforementioned Cosimo [de' Medici].
> This adder and arms are of new-planted grass in a piece
> of ground so that, the more the grass grows, the more the
> device will grow. I am not saying these things distinctly, for
> it would not be possible, since they are things which cannot
> merely be expressed, but also imagined [i.e., imaged]. And
> whoever sees them judges that they are celestial rather than
> earthly things, and everybody is agreed that this house is the
> most finished and ornate that the world has ever had or may
> have now, and that it is without comparison. In sum, it is
> believed by all that there is no other earthly paradise in the
> world than this. If Your Lordship were to see it, I take it for
> certain that it would cost you a good sum of money, because
> with the magnanimity and greatness of mind that you have,
> you too would want to do something worthy – and not only
> equal this but surpass it if that were possible. To me it seems
> like being in a new world, and I am of the opinion that in
> my days I shall never see anything worthier than this which
> I have seen and am first seeing. And not only I hold this
> opinion, but all the company here, who do nothing else but
> discuss it.

Several things about this account are striking: beyond the rhetorical hyperbole, conventional when addressing noble patrons, is the sense that to cope with his experience of the garden Niccolò needs both words (*exprimere*) and images (*imaginare*) and that even that double resource cannot capture it 'distinctly'. Partly, the garden challenges his habitual understanding of what is natural and what is artificial, so that the resolution of that paradox or *paragone* (competition) lies within the mind or imagination of the beholder, not in the garden itself; this reaction is also expressed in the claims for the Medici garden as a 'new world', another Eden, an 'earthly paradise' beyond compare. Here is – as we might say – more than meets the eye, and Niccolò's words struggle to express that extra dimension with more chance of success – a bold remark, this – than if Sforza himself were to try and re-create something physically comparable. Underlying this – a shadowy presence in so much writing about garden experience – is the hint that marvels such as the Medici garden, inherently fragmentary and transitory (we could note the stress at the start on the growth of plants), need another life in words (or images, for he also hints at the possible imagery – visual or graphic accounts – that might cope with describing the garden adequately, even though his own best efforts are verbal). Niccolò's words, it is also implied, have also been crafted in part by discussing the experience of this remarkable garden with others ('the company here'), so his is not simply a personal response.

Other early *ekphraseis* of gardens – the tradition of rendering verbally what were primarily seen as visual experiences – reveal similar emphases. Sir Henry Wotton's *Elements of Architecture* (1624), already cited in chapter Two, breaks into his succinct, spare discussion of 'a certain contrariete betweene building and gardening', which advocates regularity for the former and irregularity 'or at least . . . a very wilde Regularitie' in the latter, in order to exemplify the distinction that he is making:[3]

I have seen a garden (for the manner perchance incomparable) into which the first access was a high walk like a terrace, from whence might be taken a general view of the whole plot below but rather in a delightful confusion, then with any plain distinction of the pieces. From this the beholder descending many steps, was afterwards conveyed again, by several mountings and valings [i.e., descents], to various entertainments of his scent, and sight: which I shall not need to describe (for that were poetical) let me only note this, that every one of these diversities, was as if he had been magically transported into a new garden.

Here we have an attempt to describe, not how the site was designed or laid out (that could involve a plot or plan), but the effects of that design ('delightful confusion') upon the 'beholder'. That last term shows again the difficulty of naming those who experience gardens, because the rest of the short passage makes clear that the experience is much more than a question of beholding, involving other senses (notably 'scent'), the physical activities of climbing and descending stairways between terraces, and the bringing together in the mind of both an overview or sense of the whole and its 'diversities' or 'distinction of the pieces'. Again, as with Niccolò de' Carissimi in Florence, Wotton's very attempt to describe his experience makes its reception more important and emphatic ('poetical', 'magical') even than the designed site itself.

What is also interesting, too, about Wotton, as indeed about the next example, is that faced with what were, after all, new developments in garden design he does not focus on their formal novelties, but concentrates on how the person has experienced them. About 50 years after Wotton, Sir William Temple described another, English, garden at Moor Park in Surrey, which no longer existed in the forms he had himself witnessed. Because it has survived wholly in his recollection or reception of it ('the remembrance of what it was'), he certainly felt obliged to reconstruct its physical shape; but the description, too long to quote here,[4] is also couched in terms of his own experience of it. He notes the effects of 'use or pleasure' on its spatial organization and how the complex structure of the first two gardens – descending terraces flanked by elevated walks upon the roofs of what at the next level turn out to be arcades, 'cloisters' or *crypto-portici* – invites movement and discovery, so that it is in fact the navigation of its spaces by the visitor that seems to constitute the essence of Moor Park. Temple's description of it is certainly mediated by a concern for perambulation and – as Wotton had found in the earlier Italian example – by the site itself which seemed to dictate the process of its visitation ('as if he had been . . . transported'); the visitor at Moor Park would also have his route controlled by the spatial organization as much as by his own volition ('three descents', 'a descent by many steps flying', 'the passage into . . . ', a terrace 'three hundred paces long'). Temple, like Wotton, though at more length, ultimately offers an overview or verbal 'plot' of this garden, an experience that is available only in the retrospective spaces of the imagination; his verbal account has, though, allowed one scholar to extrapolate a ground plan from his words.[5] So that in more ways than one Moor Park comes to exist for Temple and his readers in its reception.

II

The other way of recording garden experience is of course by visual means. While nobody could confuse Wotton's or even Temple's description with either a proposal for or statement of design intention or practice, graphic work tends to be more ambiguous; it is sometimes difficult to know exactly what we are looking at. We need, then, to make some broad distinctions between kinds of visual representation and their possible motives. Some clearly arise out of the design process and emanate more or less directly from the designer; others are the result of later reactions to a built site.

In the first category, we might distinguish three possible motives. First, designers produce plans, elevations, views and structural diagrams to indicate how they expect the finished product will look and to guide workers in its fabrication (illus. 45); doubtless these would also be accompanied and glossed by verbal instructions. Very little if any of this material survives the construction site. A second kind of graphic record can be developed by the designer to further his or her own thinking about a project (illus. 46) – it was Alberti who wrote that drawing clarified his doubts as an architect, and we may assume that such work is not primarily designed for others' consumption.[6] A third mode will emerge from designers who need or wish to represent their proposals in terms that lay persons may grasp better than they do plans, sections or elevations; for instance, models or perspectival renderings can be more immediately comprehensible (illus. 47). This third mode or stage of representation is the point at

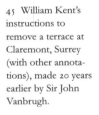

45 William Kent's instructions to remove a terrace at Claremont, Surrey (with other annotations), made 20 years earlier by Sir John Vanbrugh.

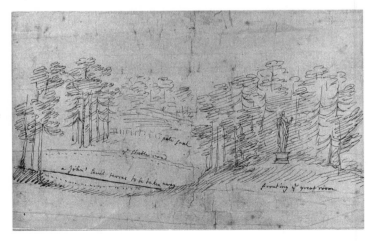

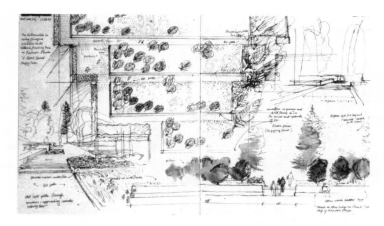

46 Laurie Olin, sketchbook page, 'clarifying thoughts for myself' for the roof garden of the LDS Assembly Building, Salt Lake City, Utah.

which a designer obviously tries to reach out to those who will primarily respond to a design – the clients who will use it – and in the process something of its afterlife has to be projected. Not all designers seem to have this concern for the reception of their work, and the scale of concern varies enormously from, say, the wonderfully sharp sketches that Lawrence Halprin made of clients in the private gardens he'd projected for them (illus. 48), or Bernard Lassus' attention to how motorists behave and could be made to respond during a stop in the countryside on a motor-way,[7] to design images empty of people or the routine collage of joggers, mothers with pushchairs and other photo-shopped imagery with which design students gesture to the afterlife of their work (illus. 49).

Representations made after the fact of the site's design and construction will be a different kind of record. Sketches, maps and (today perhaps) videos will often reveal directly, or at the very least by implication, how visitors have responded to a site, how they have tried to encode their impressions of a site that are likely to be very different when seen from a perspective other than its creator's. It is also obvious that such records will vary in usefulness enormously, depending as they do upon a

47 Laurie Olin's sketch to explain the creek and park proposed for Playa Vista, Los Angeles.

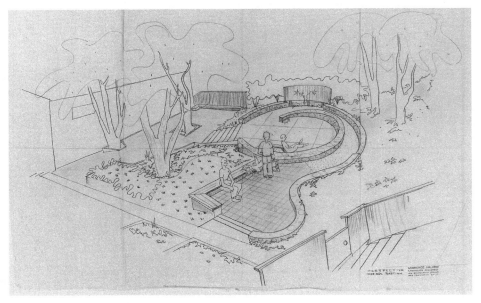

48 Lawrence Halprin, drawing of the garden for the Robert O. Bastian residence, Belvedere, California, 1950–51.

whole cluster of contingent factors, among which would be
the visitor's experience and knowledge of the specific site or of
garden art generally, and how capable they were of expressing
their reactions in word and / or image. But no surviving response
is likely to be without value, if we can adjudicate what it attempts
to record.

49 Ellen Neises,
University of
Pennsylvania School
of Design studio
project for Bosco
Gurin near Ticino,
Switzerland, 2002.

III

We have a rich documentation of such reactions for many
gardens, although they are rarely given the primacy they deserve,
partly because it is admittedly hard to know exactly how to use
them. Here, I want to look at two such sites – both from the
eighteenth century, one in England and the other in France.
Each has a different range of recorded receptions: one consists
of many visitors' accounts and a substantial body of imagery,
the other comes to us largely from its owner-creator and his
artist friends; in both, verbal accounts of visitation seem to be
at odds with the graphic evidence. One site survives in excellent
shape and is well cared for, although it has undergone considerable

transformations; the other site has long since disappeared. The history of their reception is therefore likely to be invoked in different ways because we read and view the evidence of visitors in the light of what we know about the design and re-designs of the two sites and how we have come to see their role in the longer narrative of garden history.

The reception of the gardens of Stowe, in Buckinghamshire, one of the most visible and visited 'new' gardens of the eighteenth century, constitutes a rich archive, and it has usefully been documented by George Clarke.[8] It is fair to say that Stowe provides landscape historians with prime evidence of the shift from what is generally termed 'formal' to 'informal' design; in other words, 'the whole garden history of the eighteenth century' may be deduced from Stowe.[9] This evidence consists mainly of a series of engraved maps and views that reveal the gradual release of garden spaces from the rule of geometry, 'line and level' and from the aesthetics of enclosure and boundary to more natural contours, 'pictorial' compositions and extensive sightlines into the adjacent countryside. In both its outline and its details this narrative is familiar, and as a history of design at Stowe it does not need to be challenged. Yet turning to a sampling of visitors' accounts over the same period we are confronted with materials that, while they do not question the design narrative, offer other perspectives that are just as interesting, not least because of the consistency over the first three decades of Stowe's existence of responses that plans or maps of the site could least adequately depict.

As George Clarke has rightly noted, his gathering of descriptions of Stowe comes largely from outsiders. Insiders or *habitués* would presumably be familiar with the scale of the site and the disposition of its parts within the whole, whereas it is precisely these elements that are likely to puzzle outsiders. In 1724 one such outsider, the observant Lord Perceval, noted (pp. 15–16 in Clarke's anthology) that the gardens appeared to be three times larger than they were, that even after a two-hour tour he could

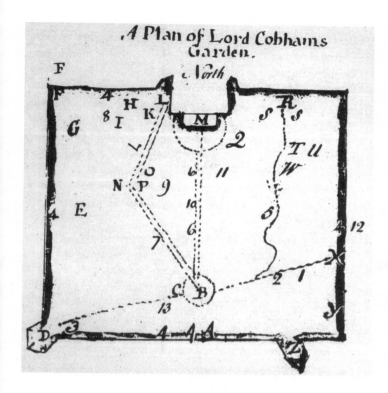

50 A sketch map
of the gardens at
Stowe,
Buckinghamshire,
drawn by an
anonymous visitor
in 1742.

not give his correspondent 'an exact Idea of this garden'; he
observes that an engraved plan would soon be available to do
precisely that, although exactly how a plan might convey a different 'Idea' from his verbal memoranda is not specified. Some visitors clearly felt that a map or plan would resolve their occasional
bafflement; one anonymous visitor of 1742 (pp. 112–17) actually
sketched his own map of the site and several ground plans of
the buildings (illus. 50), presumably as a means of relating parts
to the whole (Clarke speculates that he was a surveyor on the
lookout for design ideas for clients in East Anglia). His map
regularizes the site, schematically locating the main items within
a square of 'Grand walks' that bears little relation to either the

actual topography or the experience of movement between items; it is his written notes that give a clearer impression of how he navigated the spaces: for instance, the 'little winding shady walk' (D to B on his plan) that is a pleasant contrast to the 'great walk above it'. His main concern seems to be to obtain precise architectural descriptions and measurements of *fabriques*, but it is fascinating to see how his memoranda are also alert to items 'entertaining both the eyes and ears', to how woods suddenly 'bury' you, to the opening and closing of a serpentine walk into 'a little area', and to the fashion in which it is the garden itself that directs the visitor ('you are . . . lead by meandering walks'; 'you are led to . . .').

The multitude of buildings and statues seems to have increased the sense of prolixity, even confusion, in visitors. Perceval, having to anticipate the forthcoming plan, offers a verbal overview, stressing what he takes to be the basic characterization or 'Idea' of Stowe, namely 'a great number of walks, terminated by summer houses and heathen temples of different structure, and adorned with statues cast from the anticks'; moreover, he distinguishes between 'cross walks' that are so terminated and 'delightful . . . private ones cut thro' groves'. These notes establish a more telling version of his experience than would be obtained by cartographical precision, because he is caught up in responding to different scales of space and to the triggers and prompts of his imagination that he encounters. He also seems to be recording what he takes to be a novelty – the profusion of items that terminate vistas.

If Perceval could register the intricacies of exploration as more vital than mere ground plans would allow, another anonymous visitor, in the very same week as Perceval, seemed dedicated to the facts (p. 19). He belonged to what Charles Dickens would later call the Gradgrind school, all facts and figures, which he presumably obtained from some employee of Lord Cobham's since he would hardly have taken all the measurements himself.

It is this kind of reception, of course, that can fuel design history with its calculations, dimensions, costs and the specifics of architectural elements; equally fascinating, though, is his somewhat unexpected conclusion: true to form in noting 'fine woods 10 miles in length and 2 miles in breadth', he does comment upon the experience of passing through the woods and taking the 'prospect of the country'.

Indeed, one of the striking aspects of the reception of Stowe is the emphasis that visitors placed, not upon the gardens, but on the huge and wooded parkland that surrounded them. Noting the existence of the ha-has, Lord Perceval adduces them as further evidence of the 'beauty' of the garden's apparently inexhaustible variety, for it 'makes you ignorant how far the high planted walks extend'. Six years later, in 1730, the 8th Lord Cathcart expounded lengthily upon what his French text (pp. 28–9) called 'les Rydings' and 'le grass [i.e., *gros* or large?] Park' that was joined ('joints') to the gardens; Cathcart was an army colleague of Cobham's and therefore perhaps more interested than some in commanding a strategic map of the surrounding terrain. But others, without the military instinct, do the same: Sir John Evelyn (grandson of the diarist) writes that the 'prospect of the country is very extensive' (p. 21), while an anonymous visitor in 1742 ends his account with 'The neighbouring park is compos'd of wood and avenues, it yields such a plenty of the one and such a variety of the others, as render it highly entertaining; the Visto's open every way upon the hills and display by degrees the whole country to you' (p. 117).

These are significant acknowledgements that how visitors experienced the extensive gardens relied on what is rarely acknowledged in modern commentary, the considerably larger territory belonging to an estate of which gardens were but a part. The plan of the whole Stowe estate of 1739 (illus. 51)[10] that Charles Bridgeman's widow, Sarah, issued to accompany the engraved views of her late husband's design work within the

51 The map of
Stowe issued by
Sarah Bridgeman in
1739 to accompany
engravings of her
late husband's work
at Stowe.

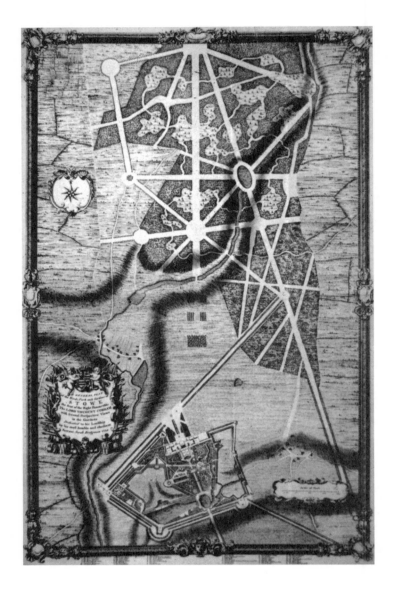

gardens acknowledged this territorial context; but rarely do modern critics show the whole plate, preferring to concentrate on the smaller, designed segment in its lower left. Contemporary viewers clearly were influenced by the surrounding territory, through which they had inevitably to pass to arrive at the inner gardens. This is not a trivial point. Our focus on the design history of the most worked segment of an estate – namely its gardens – is liable to miss how their very context in a larger landscape effected their reception. This is worth stressing these days when the surroundings of so many famous sites have lost their original and sustaining territory: at Stowe the gardens were a concentration, refinement, elaboration or epitome (to use a contemporary term) of the rural scenery on at least three levels: quite literally in the sense that trees for the gardens were derived from the estate;[11] phenomenologically in that visitors would pass from a wooded culture to a more tailored and culturated one; and symbolically in that buildings, inscriptions and statues were invoked to articulate an Englishness that drew its strengths from an appreciation of both local geography and national culture.

One other aspect of Stowe's reception is interesting: its profusion of inserted items, which Horace Walpole would famously defend in 1751 with his admiration for 'that Albano glut of buildings, let them be ever so much condemned'. Walpole's remark can be adduced in a design history as an indication among other critics (but not himself) of a declining taste for and incidence of *fabriques* in English landscapes during the eighteenth century; so too, can the testimony, three years earlier, of the Marchioness Grey (pp. 180–85). She now finds the site, unlike Lord Perceval, very predictable, even though by then the Elysian Fields had been established and the Grecian Valley projected, sizeably extending the ground plan. She tells her correspondent that, if she could draw, she'd soon convey the 'stiff set plan' of it, which was more like a public garden, lacking concealments or the private and natural turns she would have preferred. Whereas an earlier visitor had found coherence only in each segment, the Lady Grey professes to grasp the whole, and this may well be because she has had a sight of the Bridgeman map published a decade before. She admits, though, that Stowe was a surprise to her in several respects: she dislikes its aggressive sense of show, the artifice of its architectural supplements and the evident lack of 'management or beauty in the disposing' of the extensive natural features. The 'fine woods and ridings' that surround the gardens and the immediate park have much more to recommend them than the 'bare rough hills' seen as she entered the gardens. In short, it is the handling of elements throughout the site that offends her rather than their spatial disposition; it is how she received and responded during her visit, not the formality or informality of the whole, with which she is concerned. And it is worth noting that her reactions are confirmed by the *Dialogue* that William Gilpin published the very same year as Lady Grey's visit, just as they had been anticipated by many earlier visitors (as noted by Clarke, p. 180).

There are several ways in which the record of visitation at Stowe runs counter to or at least complements the design history. A gradual loosening of the geometry of organized spaces is not something, inevitably, that a single visit can register, having no opportunity to observe the garden as it evolved over the years and therefore no scope for comparisons. Nor is the primary reaction of visitors to take notice of the formal disposition at any one part; nor do the prompts or triggers at Stowe seem to have been the only means by which visitors were drawn into an understanding of it. The appreciation of the inner gardens was consciously or intuitively predicated upon a strong sense of contrast between them and the larger estate with its huge network of ridings and rich forestry, where the absence of inserted items left visitors much more to their own devices of response. Once guidebooks began to be published – the first as a brief appendix in Samuel Richardson's expansion of Daniel Defoe's *A Tour thro'*

the Whole Island of Great Britain (3rd edition, 1742), followed in
1744 by the first guidebook entirely devoted to Stowe by a local
printer and bookseller – visitors were released from identifying
each building or obtaining information from the gardeners;
what then preoccupied them was the navigation of its system
of pathways and walks, linked to but clearly not driven by what
published plans would communicate. Simultaneously, once guidebooks started to instruct in the nomenclature and even meanings of temples (see illus. 52), the visitor was further released to
explore their reactions: Defoe and Richardson, for instance,
instruct their readers on which items to prefer especially when
the 'judgement is agreeably puzzled . . . [by] so many collected
beauties' (Clarke, *Descriptions*, p. 79).

The second case study, with a less rich archive, but nevertheless offering some scope for the understanding of reception, is
Claude-Henri Watelet's garden of Moulin Joli, which survives
only in a plan, some etched views and (mainly) the owner's own
account of it in a letter to a friend in his *Essai sur les jardins*.[12]
This short work hovers generically between notes on garden
design and an affective handbook on garden behaviour or visitor
response; at times the proposals for the former are clearly subor-
dinated to their hoped-for consequences in the latter. Given that
Watelet distinguishes between the 'mechanical' and 'liberal'
aspects of garden art, he is able to downplay the practical and
technical moves, the materials and design of gardens, in favour
of their aesthetic and affective aspects, their 'appeal . . . to mind
and soul' (p. 19). Especially in his two concluding sections, on a
Chinese garden (derived at second-hand from two translations he
knew) and on his own property of Moulin Joli some years after
its establishment, it is the impact of garden art on the imagination of its visitors that interests him above all. He is not averse
to discussing design strategies, but it is their consequences that
really concern him. He even distinguishes different types of
gardens – a typical French habit of careful categorization – by

52 Page from the Stowe guidebook published by Benton Seeley (London, 1750).

Publish'd according to Act of Parliament. 1750.

Plate II.

An Artificial Peice of Rock-work.

The Temple dedicated to Venus.

An Egyptian Pyramid.

The Belvidere.

B. Seeley delin.

G. Vandergucht sculp.

the impressions they promote – 'The noble, the rustic, the agreeable, the serious, and the sad' (p. 37).

The analogy, which was current at the time and even implied by Watelet himself, is between following the plot or story of a novel and concentrating on our emotions and state of mind as we read it. Contemporary readers of Laurence Sterne's *Tristram Shandy* or *A Sentimental Journey*, for instance, would readily have appreciated the distinction and Sterne's encouragement of the second kind of reading, and it is one that the Marquis de Girardin, another French garden theorist of the time, also invokes explicitly in order to stress 'the power of landscapes on our senses and as a result on our soul'.[13] Watelet himself uses the term 'romanesque' about his preferred landscapes, a term that his modern translator correctly notes (p. 78) as occupying an etymological middle ground between 'romanesque' (fictional, having to do with novels or *romans*) and 'romantique' (our sense of romantic). In landscape architectural terms, this involves a slippage from focusing on a garden's readable imagery, plot or story to relishing the affective power that such built-in elements will have on what Girardin calls 'senses' and 'soul' and Watelet himself emotions and reveries, since (as he says) 'the heart [is] a better judge . . . than reason' (p. 69).

If part of the short *Essai* necessarily took the form of something approaching prescriptive design advice, Watelet's final account of his own Moulin Joli is significantly in the form of a 'Letter to a Friend'; written long after the moment of the garden's creation, its retrospection also colours its reading and writing of the site. These circumstances permit, or simply ensure, that the continual emphasis is on his intimate responses. From the start, when he writes of his discovery of the site while on a painting excursion from Paris, he insists on its effect on him: his eye was delighted, the topography 'produced' sensations of satisfaction, he felt 'sheltered' there (p. 60). The dilapidation of the old mill was one of its appeals, and it is the retention of that random or natural aspect that delights him after many years' work, so that the evolution of the site, its temporal dimension, becomes an essential part of its meaning for him and his friend. We should notice, too, his concern with how architectural items trigger responses: 'the sight of a small country house confirmed what I was already thinking' (p. 66), or at the end of the visit, the historic convent to which Héloïse purportedly withdrew after her affair with Abelard. Earlier in his *Essay* he had described the pleasures of the countryside as 'a fabric of desires stimulated without affectation, of satisfactions gratified without effort' (p. 26): the submerged pun on *fabriques* links those essential desires and satisfactions with the items that will provoke them. He argues that landowners should 'provide incentives for activities' to stimulate the visitor, arguing that these are always envisaged and constructed within 'a certain understanding of social mores' (pp. 49–50) as well as 'executed with enough skill and care *to awaken the desire to contemplate them*' (p. 52, my italics). Given that it is part of garden art to concentrate such imagery within its own realm, it is not surprising that Moulin Joli becomes in Watelet's version of it a place that provokes many contemplations and impressions. But even more frequent and esteemed as prompts than architectural items are inscriptions, along with the wonderful profusions of nature herself; often these are linked – an old willow speaks to Watelet and his friends in the voice of its resident 'Hamadryad', a clear example of *prosopopeia*.[14] Another inscription, 'uncertain of the mood of the person to whom it is speaking', even urges alternative reactions – 'some peace if you are sad . . . joy if you are merry'; another, rather than provoking reactions, actually records them, since it is said to have been carved there by friends after spending 'pleasant evenings discussing their interests . . .' (p. 69). However, in the final resort Watelet urges his correspondent to ignore 'mediocre verses' and 'decide for yourself' how his own curiosity can respond to the incidents of the place. His discussions of the

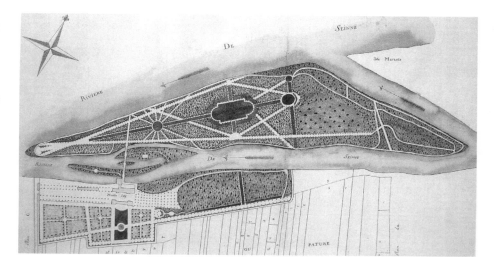

means by which the garden visitor is moved therefore runs the gamut from architectural items already in a landscape, to other structures specially inserted, to statues and inscriptions, and finally to the unprompted instincts of the human heart.

But we need to compare Watelet's written responses to Moulin Joli with other, this time graphic reactions, more interestingly a plan of the site and a group of etched imagery, mainly drawn by Watelet's artistic friends. A somewhat different version of Moulin Joli now emerges. Whoever surveyed and drew the plan (illus. 53) shows that the layout of the site invoked fairly traditional French garden imagery: there is one rectangular 'cabinet' and two 'rond-points' within the woods; almost all the paths are straight, with only the one that meanders around the northern end of one of the river islands. We might guess that the straight bridge leading from the garden area on the south across three islands would allow some oblique views of the riverscape, but as drawn it too follows an absolutely straight path. This is not the landscape of nuance and sentiment, or even of distant glimpses of the coun-tryside, that Watelet's prose describes; while the plan obviously

53 Plan of Claude-Henri Watelet's gardens at Moulin Joli, Colombes, Val d'Oise, 1780.

54 Title sheet of
six etchings of the
Moulin-Joli by
Richard de Saint-Non
after Jean-Baptiste Le
Prince, 1755.

indicated the bridges that connect bits of the property, it necessarily fails to give them the symbolic colour they acquire in his
prose, where they are seen as the very embodiment of those
bonds that friendship maintains and of what we would now term
a stream of consciousness.

With the drawings and etchings that survive (pp. 61–5), we get
yet another perspective, that of a worked and peopled landscape,
with the eponymous mill prominently displayed, which is not the
case with Watelet's prose account, but which we may presume is
his visitors responding to the item that gave the estate its name.
There is, in the first place, a set of six etchings by Richard de
Saint-Non after Jean-Baptiste Le Prince from 1755: the title sheet
(illus. 54) shows a stone block in the landscape inscribed with the
series title. Its Italian – 'Varie vedute del gentile Molino . . . ' –
implies the strong pastoral tonality that we might miss in Watelet's
prose but which, via both art work and the theatre, influenced
him greatly. The inscribed stone recalls the incidence of such
items through the site, which Waletet's prose certainly addressed,
but here foregrounds an actual example; the slab is also draped

with fishing nets and farm tools, and a diminutive figure leans
on its rear, but not in a way that would enable him to read its
inscription; presumably we see him rather as indigenous inhabitant than curious visitor. The remaining five images all deploy
the appropriate staffage – fishermen in a boat on the river, a
family by the water's edge, cowherds and shepherds. These
incidents certainly reflect elements of Watelet's description, most
notably they give us graphic recollections of the natural elements
of the site and some of the crucial built items that trigger
responses; they also declare his fondness for a peopled and
worked landscape; but as in three other drawings the 'visitor' is
necessarily distanced from the scene, his 'role' being taken often
by small figures gazing into the scene from the foreground with
their backs towards us. The vague sense of dilapidation, the
traces of time-worn buildings and land, is there, but the nostalgia
of retrospection that constitutes so much of Watelet's reception
of his own garden is missing. One particular drawing by Hubert
Robert (illus. 55), who helped Watelet design his landscape,
reveals the Mill and one of the bridges, with two tiny figures at

55 Hubert Robert,
drawing of the
Moulin Joli.

the water's edge: it could be both a projection of how the scene would look when work was finished or be a fond record of how the site strikes one of its familiar, intimate visitors.

The visual record is invaluable, yet we need to have it intersect with Watelet's account of its reception by himself and his friend to get a full picture of Moulin Joli. The intimacy that was clearly an essential part of the place can perhaps be suggested by the delicately etched texture and the scale of the figures; but the whole repertoire of emotions and sentiments, of course, is not released by the graphic imagery, and we need Watelet's prose to gloss the associations of the visual scenery. Yet the staffage figures, our surrogates in these graphic representations, do however imply indirectly by their stance and direction of their gaze the involvement of those visitors. One element that the visual artists manage to suggest more strongly than Watelet needed or wanted to do in his prose is the sense of a place defined and shaped by the social activities it harbours; this is done partly by suggestions of Dutch and Flemish genre subjects. And, finally, it is surely important to accept that the associative narrative of Watelet's ramble through his property was provoked by a layout that, judging solely from the plan, we would not necessarily imagine as designed to engage its visitors in the way he so happily describes. Yet Watelet's point of view is confirmed by one other verbal account that has come down to us: the Prince de Ligne, an enthusiastic and well-travelled gardenist, reported on his visit to the Moulin Joli. Much as he was always interested in design elsewhere and in the formal moves of a layout, at Moulin Joli he neglects almost entirely to describe the site, apart from objecting to 'the prettiest unreason' of the 'Dutch bridge'. Instead he celebrates the 'panorama of your soul' that Moulin Joli opens for him through the range and swirl of emotions ('Regrets, joys, desires, all will rush upon you at once'); in particular he urges visitors to meditate – be prompted by – 'the inscriptions that Taste has placed there'.[15]

IV

There are clearly – and unsurprisingly – considerable differences between visual and verbal records of reception, just as reception itself opens up alternative ways of understanding gardens. By the end of the eighteenth century these differences came to be an interesting issue in the experience of gardens. It was no coincidence that this was also the time that saw the rise and theorization of the so-called Picturesque garden, since the traditions that gave rise to it made much of the collaboration of word and image: its leading exponent and popularizer, William Gilpin, was even hailed as the master of the 'pen and pencil united'.[16] Contrariwise, it was also the time that the German critic Gotthold Ephraim Lessing chose famously to distinguish between the resources and achievements of verbal and visual media.[17] These are complicated theoretical matters, but we can see them in practice and with some clarity in the books of two garden commentators, Thomas Whately and Joseph Heely, whose works we have already encountered.

When Thomas Jefferson visited English gardens in 1786 he took with him a copy of Whately's *Observations on Modern Gardening* (1770). As its title implied, this was the most up-to-date account of recent developments in garden design; but it also explained how the new designs might be experienced. I assume today that either we do not question how to visit a garden or, if conscious of the activity, we think that we know how to visit Stowe, say, or Painshill; but it was probably not so obvious or predictable for a man of Jefferson's time, confronted with exciting and novel modes of laying out the land. Whately's book was in part addressed to such visitors, combining suggestions on how to experience the new gardens with design precepts (he hardly descends to instructions, which were becoming the province of much more practical manuals). The segments of his book that deal with the experience of modern gardens are cast in the form of verbal descriptions, which occupy very roughly a third of his text.

Whately insists upon the importance of these passages when his title-page declares that the book is 'Illustrated by Descriptions'. Indeed, the volume in all of its first five editions is completely devoid of engraved plates, somewhat surprising for its date, since by then there was a considerable fund of both engraved views of country seats as well as a publishing tradition of illustrated books on gardens. It was only in 1801 that Whately's sixth edition was provided with some (fairly unimpressive) engravings, yet it still retained the phrase 'Illustrated by Descriptions' on the title-page. It may be that Whately or his publisher could not at first afford engraved plates, and that is certainly the more likely explanation in the case of Heely's *Letters on the Beauties of Hagley, Envil and The Leasowes* (1777), which also had no illustrations. Whately certainly told his French translator, who wished to illustrate the Paris edition (1771), that even 'mediocre engravings' required 'much trouble and expense' and that they would be far worse than the 'most beautiful perspectives in nature' and were therefore best avoided.[18] But that very explanation, along with Whately's insistence on his title-page that the book was 'Illustrated by Descriptions', is striking. 'Perspectives' was a word that referred at the time to graphic representations – in other words pictures that nature herself created (with or without the aid of a designer). By translating these pictures into words Whately – like Heely after him – was privileging the experience or reception of gardens and landscapes over their design or formal elements.

There are three ways to explain Whately's and Heely's determination to translate pictures or 'perspectives in nature' into words. They were invoking Classical ideas about the relations between the arts that were epitomized both in Horace's catchphrase, *ut pictura poesis*, whereby paintings could be read as texts and literary texts imagined as pictures or sculpture, and in the related rhetorical tradition of *ekphrasis* – verbalizing the visual, describing graphic representations in words. Or, they were participating in the later, Renaissance fascination with the different capabilities of the arts – the *paragone* – and were showing that words could do better than graphic representations; this topic reached something of a climax in 1766, just four years before Whately, with the publication in Germany of Lessing's *Laokoön*, and with the popular writings of Diderot in France, where his commentaries on Salon pictures conducted his readers verbally into the imagined spaces of the painted imagery.[19] The third motive, shared in different ways by both Lessing and Diderot, was to articulate the experience or reception of art; in the case of Whately and Heely this was new, cutting-edge garden art. All three explanations are surely involved, but the two traditional devices of *ekphrasis* and *paragone* are now brought in aid of a distinctly modern fascination with experience.

Whately's 'descriptions' are of both un-designed, but prime, Picturesque sites, such as the Wye Valley and the Derbyshire Dales, and of a cluster of important modern gardens, principally Blenheim, Claremont, Esher, Hagley, Persefield, The Leasowes, Stowe and Woburn. His *ekphraseis* attempt to convey the full scope of these landscapes, including the design inspiration from paintings and engravings, how visual encounters were to be translated into words and, ultimately, the homage thereby rendered to the direct garden experience itself. Whately insinuates that only in his careful descriptions can the experience of landscape come fully into being. Indeed, he actually thought gardens were 'as superior to landskip painting as a reality to a representation', and consequently he was equally firmly committed to an experience in gardens for the articulation of which the verbal was apparently superior to the graphic. Hence his commitment to 'illustrate' sites only 'with descriptions'; the verbal is equated with the real ('reality') and the graphic with visual representations. He was thus in agreement with his French counterpart, the

Marquis de Girardin, otherwise a staunch defender of the painterly model for landscape design, who considered that the 'character' of a particular garden scene spoke to the imagination and the heart in ways that privileged the poet over the painter in its recording.[20]

Whately's descriptions combine two modes of reception: that which grasps the whole site, and that which responds to its individual segments (the debt to painting is clear, since a fine painting carefully relates its parts to the whole composition, formally and thematically). The implication is that, while negotiating a garden bit by bit, we must keep the idea of the whole site in our minds, for which mental picture words provide a necessary *ekphrasis* (as opposed to maps – though Whately does not go as far as to say that). As the visit to a garden unfolds, specific or local views – say from the Temple of Venus at Stowe, or from the Gothick Pavilion at Painshill – are admired for their combination of completeness and detail, overall character, or what he calls 'consistency preserved in the midst of variety'.

Whately's tone is largely generalizing, especially when he offers these overviews; we tend, as a result, to miss how much they are nonetheless examples of reception. But when he engages with local spaces within a landscape, he begins to register more personal or subjective responses – momentary effects of light in the Elysian Fields at Stowe, or the appreciation of some formal moment of landscape composition. Here too words are primary, best suited to articulate these private pictures in the head. Subtly enough, Whately's prose enacts the visitor's conscious and explicit recognition of design effects: the eminence with which the Gothick belvedere at Painshill 'exhibits a landskip distinguished from the last in every particular'. And the visitor's eye is tracked as it takes in precisely and carefully each item in that natural perspective – the artificial lake at the base of the slope, its islands, a distant wood to the right, a hermitage, a lofty tower, and so on. Once Whately embarks on the actual perambulation, it is the changing moods provoked by the scenic passage that absorb him – cheerful, calm, animated, 'not dreary, not romantic, but rude'. Similarly at Stowe, a landscape much more cluttered with buildings and readable objects, Whately is alert to them singly and in relation to each other: in the Elysian Fields the 'multiplicity of objects both within and without, which embellish and enliven the scene, give it a gaiety, which the imagination can hardly conceive, or the heart wish to be exceeded'. Sometimes the discrimination of a particular character or mood at a given spot seems to us both obsessive and trivial; but it implies how much the accomplished visitor was expected to adjudicate the designed effects, remark on them aloud to his or her companions, write them in a diary or simply rehearse them in his or her head.

But *ekphrasis* is not an end in itself. One of its perhaps paradoxical ambitions is to use verbal description to take the reader back into the fullest experience of the visual object, in the case of gardens that means putting the reader back, as it were, into the garden picture. In this manoeuvre, words offer to displace / replace themselves with the whole immediate experience of the actual thing described, an experience that involves all the senses, the mind and the imagination. It is as if the ecphrasist says 'Look' rather than read.[21] No wonder Whately's book was used as a guidebook by Jefferson and others; even armchair travellers could feel that they were transported into the places described. In another important fashion, too, *ekphrasis* is not merely a rhetorical trope, but the sign of 'a social discourse on art and its viewing';[22] in other words, it is not so much that it shows off literary skills in making palpable to a reader the visual experience as it declares a society's expectations about (in our case) the viewing and experiencing of gardens. One was meant to translate the formal effects, what one saw, into more elaborate and expressive modes, partly because the garden was not considered only a visual experience, even by the most dedicated of its

Picturesque exponents, but a cultural, social and political affair as well.

Whately's illustrative descriptions manage, furthermore, to capture the best of both of the worlds that his German contemporary Lessing wished to separate. If Lessing found painting best equipped to communicate static visual properties and writing to deal with motion and process, then an accomplished *ekphrasis* does both. Its own verbal medium allows the record of temporality, sounds, activity, motion and emotion, while its pretence to imitate the stillness of paintings additionally brings into play colours, form, spatial relationships and other visible aspects.[23] Whately responds to both the painterly possibility – the set views – in gardens and to the different pleasures that come from movement through their spaces. Indeed, he is at his most interesting when he insists on the passage through different sceneries. This emphasis on the process of visitation not only effectively endorses his distinction between and preference for real landscapes over painted ones, but makes more compelling his reluctance to have his book illustrated with what would inevitably have been static engravings. His preference for expression or expressiveness in a landscape design over what he calls emblems – fixed, contrived, allegorical elements – is also part of his refusal of the pictorial in favour of what he terms the 'transitory'.[24] The full recognition of these 'transitory' experiences grants more power and effect to their verbal translations. We do not have to reach ahead to a modern phenomenologist like Maurice Merleau-Ponty to appreciate the Picturesque connoisseur 'interlacing himself with the world [in ways] which [were] recorded in its process of appearing to perception'.[25]

That modern anticipation notwithstanding, Whately is a very eighteenth-century writer in his observance of the decorum or genre of manual or treatise that he has principally chosen, so that – as his title-page insists – the ecphrastic passages do in fact stand out as a response to recent landscaping that is different

from design precepts. Other genres – like epistolary correspond-
ence – would offer greater opportunities and greater freedoms
for the narration of mental and emotional reactions to scenery.
That is precisely the move that Heely makes in his eponymous
Letters, and the contrast between the two writers is instructive,[26]
especially as Whately himself described The Leasowes (nine
pages) and Hagley (twelve pages; Hagley was incidentally chosen
for an illustration in his sixth edition). Heely is far more attentive
to the psychological process of a garden visit than how that site
might have been designed in the first place. Where real physical
or objective prompts – temples, inscriptions, statuary – are far
less frequent, as was the case in all three sites in contrast to, say,
Stowe or Painshill, Heely focuses on triggers and prompts that
exist in the visitor's imagination, on the inner landscape that
unfolds as a counterpart to the actual stroll. Words are for him
an essential vehicle of that experience and its record.

Yet the climate of publishing from Whately's and Heely's day
right up to our own has proved too strong to be resisted, and
illustrated garden books have become the norm, not to say *de
rigueur*. They were perhaps fighting a losing battle in a garden
world where the fine accomplishments of *ekphrasis* were no
longer appreciated, where the transposable possibilities of *ut
pictura poesis* were neglected, and where the Renaissance fascination with the *paragone* ceased to be of concern, and where the
technology of book production would permit frequent and not
too expensive illustration. Typical of this new climate is the second edition of George Mason's *An Essay on Design in Gardening*,
published in 1795, 27 years after its first appearance. It now
contained a section entitled 'A Revisal [i.e., review] of some
late publications on gardening', which addressed Whately's
Observations among other works. Mason dismissed its 'descriptions', mocking what he calls their 'supernumary words'.[27] Yet at
the same time he is exceptionally – and I might say inevitably –
alert to the characteristics of landscape for which painterly or

visual imagery is inadequate – in short, he really needs words to translate the experience of change, growth, decay and their role in establishing the particular character of a scenery. He argues 'the insufficiency of paintings to instruct a gardener', partly because in reality our lateral vision is far more extensive than can be conveyed by a graphic representation. His scepticism about some of what are in the twenty-first century taken as the only constituents of the Picturesque is well taken; yet he deprives himself of the opportunity to use verbal descriptions as a means of evading or augmenting the restrictions of a painterly imitation.[28]

We might conclude by remarking, however, that Whately and Heely seem nonetheless to have succeeded in establishing the role of words in garden experience to such an extent that publications ever since theirs have come to rely as much upon the verbal as the visual. The published works of William Gilpin and Humphry Repton are two obvious examples of this double reliance; more intriguing is the series of what are basically collections of engravings of country seats, by William Watts, William Angus and William Birch in the years between 1779 and 1791,[29] which nevertheless also invoke texts to gloss, if minimally, their graphic images. And when we come to the enormous corpus of books on gardens, garden-making and garden sensibility that continue to emerge from publishing houses to this day, we have to acknowledge that the joint enterprise of word and image continues to flourish, if not always convincingly.

SIX

The Role of Movement in Garden Reception

tarry with secure delight, or saunter with perpetual amusement
THOMAS WHATELY

the first principle behind the layout of promenades and gardens is . . .
to combine constantly objects that arouse our curiosity and compel
us to move about with objects that fix our attention and invite us
to linger
CLAUDE-HENRI WATELET [1]

It is clear from several crucial sources canvassed so far in these
essays – the *Hypnerotomachia Poliphili*, Wotton and Temple,
Watelet's narrative of Moulin Joli or Gilpin's tour of Stowe in
the *Dialogue* – that movement is an essential experience in every
garden visit.[2] We need accordingly to explore more carefully how
a poetics of movement can contribute to an adequate understanding of garden reception. While it is true that the Picturesque
garden – despite its name and an erroneous modern reputation
for merely static, scenic views – most emphatically encouraged
and relied on the visitor's movement through its spaces, older
gardens also depended on motion as a crucial factor in their
reception. While analysis of movement may be a modern concern,[3] an awareness of its contribution to garden or landscape
experience is considerably older. Both Poliphilo and the lover in
Le Roman de la rose learn only by the very process of accumulating

experience as they wander through different landscapes; these are early instances of what have been called 'psychogeographical readings' of place.[4] Sir Henry Wotton's albeit brief commentary on a late sixteenth-century Italian garden reveals how transport in both its senses – motion and emotion – guides his reactions. Sir William Temple learns or explains the incremental scales of handling art and nature by his progress through three zones of Moor Park, in the same way that visitors to Stowe in the next century found its gardens the more remarkable because of their coming upon them after traversing impressive and extensive woodlands.

Many landscape designers will aim to promote or at least permit certain kinds of movement, of which we might provisionally identify three – a ritual walk or procession, a stroll and a ramble. But once physical spaces have been laid out, their visitors may opt, for various reasons, to move through a site against the grain of its own invitations (hence those occasional notices that ask visitors to keep to the path!). Or the layouts themselves may induce or provoke visitations that the designer did not or could not have anticipated; so when Wotton notices how the ups and downs of the terraced Italian hillside 'transported' him rather than allowing him to determine his own route, we are witness of the surrender by a sensitive visitor to the demands of a site that probably go beyond the design's establishment of terracing and hydraulic display. Watelet, who spends a good part of his *Essai sur les jardins* discussing movement and the associations it promotes, observes that what distinguished a painting from a real landscape design is that the 'Person viewing picturesque scenery in a [modern] park, changes their organization by changing his location, and may often fail to move or pause according to the intentions of the composition' (p. 36); moreover, if the paths and roads are 'appropriately laid out', those persons' feet will lead them to where their own 'desire' can be sustained and satisfied (pp. 36–7). This is being moved by a garden in the fullest sense, which one assumes should be the effect of all great landscape experiences: they are larger than the vision of any one designer or visitor. Yet movement and its attendant pauses, in fact, can create a landscape experience unique to one particular stroller. Certainly, no modern visitor to Versailles negotiates the Petit Parc in anything like the way its creator / patron, Louis xiv, envisaged, or even that followed by a member of the court circle like Madame de Scudéry; today's visitors make of Versailles, as they would of many other historical sites, different, personal and often valid receptions.

A small example of how a design may, without itself being altered in any way, elicit different reactions will highlight the significance for a reception of gardens of different responses to the same layout or structure. First think of a feature that could be found in many seventeenth-century gardens: an arcade or row of regular arches, in front of which – say at a distance of two-and-a-half metres – is planted a line of trees, perhaps pruned to seem somewhat architectural and certainly with each tree positioned directly in front of every upright element in the arcade; it is an image of control and order that is registered well in ground plan or by a visitor directly *en face*. Then imagine walking slowly along and *across* this feature, outside the line of trees and looking past their trunks towards the sequence of arches; what in plan or section would seem very rigid, regular and 'formal' becomes a far less schematic montage of modulating shapes – lines, angles, openings, shadows, all constantly changing. This precise experience of what is termed *parallax* was discussed in 1764 by Julien-David Leroy to exemplify the 'series of much varied views' that a perambulating spectator will enjoy,[5] and it suggests how fresh habits of viewing and thinking, promoted by movement, can appropriate older designs and make them new.

Wotton addresses the imperatives of movement on several occasions in his *Elements of Architecture*. In a political metaphor that acknowledges both the sovereign rights of the eye – traditionally supreme among the five senses – and its dangerous capacity to take over and dominate, he links sight with the desire and need to move:

> a well-chosen prospect . . . I will call the royalties of sight. . . . There is lordship likewise of the eye (as of the feet) which being a ranging and imperious, and (I might say) an usurping sense; can endure no narrow circumscription, but must be fed, both with extent and variety.[6]

Here, too, we may sense that movement, prompted by what the eye sees, can 'usurp' or override the design intentions of a given site. But how can designers dictate the kinds of movement that visitors should adopt in their parks and gardens? As Watelet notes and Humphry Repton later in England would practise, paths and roads are crucial: obviously the designer's choice of the width, grade, lateral elements, route and underfoot texture will determine in some measure how paths are used. Width will determine how many people can walk abreast, thereby ensuring sociability or intimacy; steepness or grade will effectively impact how and at what speed a site is experienced, but this can be adjusted by the simple expedient of the path's following a less direct route up or down a slope; the size of gravel has an immediate effect on how fast one can walk along it (though that will also depend on our footwear). Paths by definition also follow a pre-assigned route, and how and where they conduct the visitor will be directly responsible for what triggers and prompts he or she will encounter along the way, whether these are inserted items of sculpture and architecture or 'natural features' found along the route like ponds and waterfalls. But beyond these material means by which a visitor may be manipulated, the history of garden design also indicates that there are perhaps other mechanisms and motives that a designer might embrace and devise; these affect the mental and imaginative ways in which a landscape is experienced. Three essential kinds of visitation suggest themselves.

I

The procession is a ritual movement that follows a preordained path and purpose, which is, on account of its prescription, repeatable on innumerable occasions; indeed, reiteration is expected. Ritual movement can take advantage of a pre-existing site, but more usually one is laid out or modified specifically for the event it accommodates. The route – that is, the path, the movement along it and its reasons and objectives – is encoded, its prescriptions laid down in some formal record such as social or religious convention or written text (like a liturgy), the following of which implicit or explicit guidelines constitutes the performance of that ritual. It is likely to be undertaken collectively by a group that follows an orderly sequence of moves and does so on special occasions, whether designated festivals, *ad hoc* fêtes or social events. However, a solitary version of procession or ritual walk in which one person consciously sets him- or herself to follow a path established and even endorsed by long-term collective usage is also a possibility. This mode of movement, then, implies a specific route with designated paths and activities, all culturally validated, and with some higher objective than the mere performance and with a wider reference than the site of the ritual itself.

Examples of such sites where the design has dictated visitors' ritual movements and therefore their experience include the *sacri monti* of northern Italy (illus. 56), the Versailles of Louis xiv and his court, the Jardin Monceau created for the Duc de Chartres from 1773, a highly visible landscape like Stowe once the publication of guidebooks organized its visitation, and an equally famous, cult-like modern garden such as Sissinghurst or Giverny. In all these instances the organization of experience is calculated to remind visitors of previous and exterior events: the *sacri monti*, for example, are landscaped versions of the stations of the cross, designed to recall or represent, however indexically, the

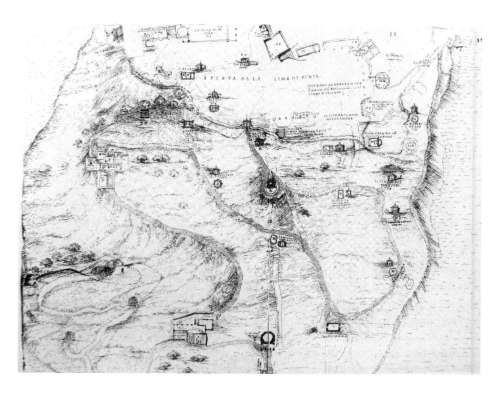

56 Map of the *sacro monte* at Varallo, from Galeazzo Alessi, *Libro dei misteri* (1565–9).

topography of Jerusalem through which Jesus carried his cross towards Calvary. This sequence need not of course have landscaped forms – the stations of the cross within a Catholic church have no relation to any topography except the given spaces of the ecclesiastical structure, nor does the sequence need special layouts, since actual urban sites can be invoked to recall Jerusalem and to perform what has been termed stational liturgy.[7]

Whatever route was taken around Versailles, and there were variations authorized by the Sun King himself, the site constantly alluded to the status, exploits and political activities of its monarch, as the fictional visitors in Scudéry's *Promenade de Versailles* constantly declare ('while praising Versailles we turned naturally to speaking about the king'[8]). In three different manu-

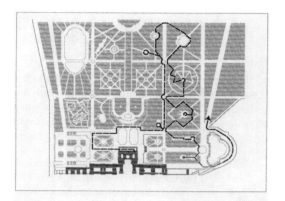

57 Route maps of
Versailles in Louis
XIV's guidebooks of
1689, 1691 and
1702–4.

1691 et 1695

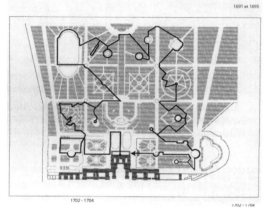

1702 - 1704

1702 - 1704

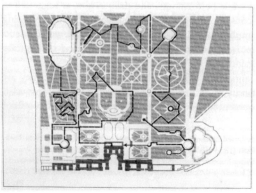

151

scripts (illus. 57) Louis himself dictated how people should view the Versailles gardens: he told them to turn left or right, where to pause and 'consider' ('there a pause will be made in order to consider the ramps'[9]); but exactly what considerations the visitor would entertain at any one spot are not spelt out, presumably because these would be self-evident rather than that visitors were being left to their own devices. But even if they were, these individual reactions would have been programmed within a set order of visit.

Louis's simple directions are of a piece with the elaborate *fêtes* that were mounted in his gardens in 1664, 1668 and 1674. Predicated upon a focused, formal and processional movement through selected parts of the grounds, the function of these social rituals-cum-theatrical showpieces was to display the great qualities of the monarch. The difference between them and Louis's guidebooks is that they were elaborately scripted, amplified and conducted with more control. Suppers, ballets, tilts, dramatic presentations and fireworks were presented in different parts of the garden, which was modified or finished specifically for the event, and between which locations the audience moved. But the ritual also derived strength both from the fashion in which courtiers were both actors and spectators, and from the official enshrining of each fête in print and letterpress.[10]

The rituals of Giverny, as befit a modern garden, have much to do with the commercialism and commodification of culture. They derive from the immense popular esteem for Impressionist painting and in particular Monet's own celebration of his garden in innumerable and endlessly reproduced paintings. Similarly, Sissinghurst vibrates both with its own fame and reputation that are antecedent to any visit and with the associations established with its creators through a concentrated body of memoir and, like Giverny, a kind of a secular hagiography. What amounts to a ritual visitation at these two gardens proceeds from a combination of the hype of promotional tourism with

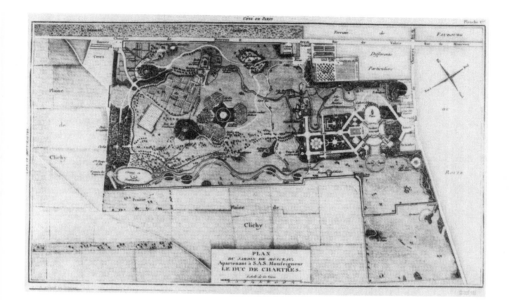

58 Plan of the Jardin Monceau, Paris, from Carmontelle's book on this site, 1779.

their deserved and now legendary reputation as preternatural examples of horticultural fecundity and flair.

Either the physical organization of these sites or the ritual movement through them (including the attitudes taken up by visitors) also suggest that a full processional route does not have to be followed in its entirety; segments can be undertaken, sections taken in different order, although always in the confidence that the whole system is in place and gives meaning to the fragment. The Jardin Monceau (illus. 58) strung out along a constantly changing itinerary a series of representations that its designer Carmontelle called 'tous les temps et tous les lieux';[11] a visitor could clearly sample some of these in the knowledge that a fuller repertoire of times and places was still available. However, the initial sections of Monceau seem to have constituted something of a even more rigorous, perhaps Freemasonic initiation sequence: entrance was through a

Chinese gateway, then past a Gothick laboratory to one side and a pavilion on the other, eventually reaching a mirrored wall; pressing a button, the visitor gained admission into an elaborate winter garden of exotic effects terminating in a grotto where dinner was served and music played in a chamber overhead; passing out from here, the visitors discovered themselves in a farmyard.

Carmontelle issued a description of this elaborate site, in effect a guide through each and every element of its itinerary; in one sense he was simply ensuring that the layout was accorded a reception worthy of and fully alert to his design invention. One important task of every guidebook is to ensure that we miss nothing of importance. But their use also has the effect, even today, of ritualizing a garden visit, although few such publications derive from their creators like Carmontelle or patrons like Louis XIV (however, at Versailles today visitors may apparently hire an audio cassette in which the voice of Louis XIV purportedly guides them!). Guidebooks lead and instruct, ensuring that the majority of visitors will follow the same route, observe and understand the same things, and so begin to constitute something like a ritual visitation. We can see this process at work during the eighteenth century at Stowe, where the fame of the gardens drew visitors from abroad as well as England; early visitors struggled to make sense of the extensive layout, but insiders such as Gilbert West and then commercial booksellers produced materials for distribution and sale that had the effect of channelling all visitors along predetermined routes. The youthful William Gilpin used one of these published guidebooks at Stowe in 1747, and his published *Dialogue* shows how much his visit took on the character of a ritual as a result. But his *Dialogue*, as befits its format, also reveals an alternative impulse, succumbing to distractions of a less programmed sort as one of his characters subverts the processional guidance of the other. Today, when the Stowe gardens, after being for many years in the charge of Stowe School, are now managed by the National Trust, guidebooks published by each institution authorized different itineraries that accorded with the management needs of these two bodies; people who have used or use either will in consequence have a significantly different perspective on their visit.[12]

Guidebooks are essentially a modern product, responding to the growing taste for tourism and its ritualistic aspects. But something equivalent did exist in the Renaissance,[13] and these poetical celebrations or descriptions would have promoted the reputations and prestige of princely and aristocratic owners who clearly wanted their gardens to speak fully and appropriately to visitors as well as to those who would read them as armchair travellers; one consequence would be that all visitors who used these texts would share a response. In Roman times Pliny the Younger wrote two letters describing his villa gardens to friends; historians rightly rely on these as valuable indications of how the sites were laid out, but they are also to be read as one owner's concern to have his properties experienced in what he thought a proper and apt sequence; it is surely possible that his letters, careful rhetorical inventions though they are, follow the structure of actual visits when he showed off his estates to actual visitors.[14]

We may even see another form of conducted tour in the narrative of *Le Roman de la rose*, where the dreamer is assisted through the gardens by various figures who are required to explain and instruct him. The rituals of courtly love are learned and performed by following a journey through the allegorical spaces of an imaginary garden (although one that must have contained some familiar elements if only to ensure that contemporary readers readily followed the narrative): the lover knocks on doors, crosses thresholds, enters enclosures, meets strangers. He knows where he is and what he has to do because of his immediate location or because some figure he has encountered (a 'genius of the place') explains its significance.

The poem is a lesson in the rituals of courtship, so that anyone who finds himself in a similar 'garden' may know how to conduct himself.[15] The analogies with actual garden processionals are clear, and it is not too much of a stretch to compare the help the lover receives along the way to the provision of information to curious or baffled visitors by gardeners or other insiders in large gardens like Stowe before the advent of guidebooks.

II

To ritual movement may be opposed both the stroll and the ramble, although important differences exist between them; a stroll may be thought of as a middle term between processional and ramble. It is clear that in processional or ritualistic designs,

the visitor's experience is strongly controlled if not in some measure dictated. What distinguishes the stroll and the ramble from the processional walk (leaving aside the possibility that visitors may choose to ignore the ritualistic demands of a site) is the illusion that this control may not be there so strongly or at all; as a consequence a visitor is allowed some initiative, because less is expected of him or her; he or she may even feel wholly in charge of how the site is experienced.

The stroll garden is most famously identified with Chinese design (illus. 59), but may also be said to have come into its own with the western Picturesque garden. The stroll implies an ultimate purpose within a site and a sense both of destination – as with the strolling musician who moves about while performing – and of deliberation, as suggested in the word *saunter*, which implies self-conscious activity and even some anticipation of

59 Tang Yifen (1778–1853), untitled landscape drawing, hand-scroll, ink and wash.

being watched by others. Strolling also implies a defined route between whatever incidents punctuate and give rhythm to the movement. As a pastime it tends to be a small group activity, but individuals may also engage in it.

Rambles, on the other hand, entail movement with no obvious external prompt; they are promoted largely by the will or curiosity of an individual enjoying the leisure to wander and finding a territory in which to do that: the Dadaists called this 'deambulation', which Francesco Careri has dubbed 'a sort of automatic writing in real space'.[16] Ramble was the term adopted by Frederick Law Olmsted and Calvert Vaux for a section in Central Park that was composed of meandering routes among rocks and densely planted trees and shrubs (see illus. 19); it was a term also used during the 1850s for a segment of the Picturesque community of Llewellyn Park, New Jersey, and it had its formal predecessor in the squiggly paths between axial avenues indicated on early eighteenth-century ground plans of English estates (in 1718 Stephen Switzer called these a 'private and natural turn'[17]). Unlike the slightly more social implication of stroll (perhaps evidenced by such broad avenues or promenades as the Mall in Central Park), ramble clearly came into vogue at a time when pedestrian exercise, walking and hiking became popular, and individual versions of the hike seemed less eccentric and more acceptable. However, as early as 1724 at Stowe Lord Perceval, in distinguishing between 'cross walks' terminated with buildings and 'private walks cut thro' groves', seems to be assigning two different modes of exploration.[18]

Rambles are for the pleasures of movement itself, without definite purpose or preordained routes or destinations; a ramble implies impulse, spontaneity, a disconnected wandering, and therefore it is more likely to be undertaken in solitude, since one person's disconnections would distract from another's. Nor does one need actual paths for rambling, since this mode of movement could take place across any open space without obstacles,

like the Long Meadow of Prospect Park, Brooklyn (illus. 60).
Joseph Heely in 1777 criticized the introduction of too many
paths by saying that when he visited a site he did not think of
himself as 'journeying – I walk there to enjoy, and to admire
their variety – to linger in every sense, and trace the pencil in all
its touches'.[19] Not only does rambling imply an infinite variety of
routes, when visitors never follow the same track every time, it
presupposes a dedication to changing the pattern of exploration
at each visit to a specific site; and where no paths are indicated,
there is no guarantee that even the same visitor will ramble along
the very same route every time. The ramble tends also to elim-
inate visual clues by which a walk might be structured: thus the
Long Meadow of Prospect Park or the more extensive spaces

60 The Long
Meadow, Prospect
Park, Brooklyn,
New York.

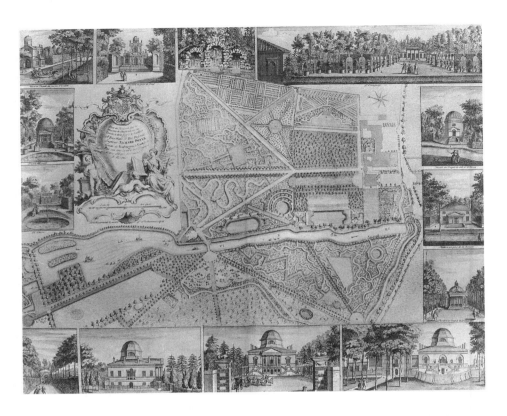

61 John Rocque's engraved plan of Chiswick House, Middlesex, 1736.

of 'Capability' Brown's greensward, such as the hillside that slopes down towards Longleat House from Heaven's Gate, do not propose any specific course to be plotted across their open landscapes; even if there were paths, the rambler is just as likely to opt for alternative ways of crossing such open territory. Thus the ideal grounds for rambling are a natural or naturalistic topography. But forms of the natural are culturally determined, so that Olmsted's Ramble or the squiggly paths within the arms of the *pattes-d'oie* at Chiswick in the 1730s were at each time offered as artless, 'wild' and unprogrammed sectors (today, of course, they seem contrived [illus. 61]). Yet in the final resort ramblers within a designed landscape, however extensive, may be confident that their aimless wandering will eventually bring them to some familiar or safe spot where they can take their bearings. Hikers may get lost if they are unwise enough to ramble in the White Mountains of New Hampshire or on Dartmoor, which would not be the case in the Labyrinth at Hampton Court or the wooded valleys of The Leasowes.

Strolls require the same confidence in plotted and designed spaces, but with more prominent cues and prompts, as well as more strongly controlled routing and sight lines. The stroll gardens of China, sites such as Stourhead (illus. 62) and Painshill, or some of the more social spaces of modern public parks, have been contrived to give strollers incentives for moving forward. These incentives are either a clearly designated path, a series of

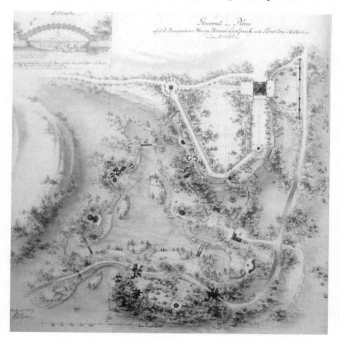

62 F. M. Piper, map of the lakeside gardens at Stourhead, Wiltshire, 1779.

63 A path through
a nature reserve,
New Jersey.

events and incidents along that path, or usually both. These can
include temples, pavilions, sculpture, seats or benches, inscriptions, urns, drinking fountains – anything in short to allow some
forward momentum and satisfaction at the completion of each
segment. They are seen or glimpsed and so pull the feet forward;
but equally they work by the simple expedient of inspiring
confidence that something lies ahead to be discovered, just as
the strolling player heads for a village with the assurance that
some barn will be available for storming. Sites designed with
these built-in inducements range from the Italian garden through
which Wotton was conveyed by 'various entertainments' to the
modern nature reserve (illus. 63), where visitors find well-defined
paths that wind through territory dotted with informational
signage and seats for rest and contemplation.

The expectation of finding things on a stroll is likely to be
culturally derived. As a visiting Englishman, Wotton was obviously
learning how to surrender to an Italian garden's 'entertainments'.
Chinese stroll gardens presuppose that the pathway, however
meandering, will deliver pleasure and stimulation of mind, senses

and imagination.[20] The European visitor to a Picturesque garden was conditioned to expect the incorporation of follies, *fabriques* or studied viewpoints worth discovering, even if they were not immediately discernible. Today, garden visitors either know to continue on the stroll for the same reason – that they understand the opportunities (botanical, architectural or imaginative) of a given site – or they follow a guide or map that entails the same promise of discovery (albeit alerting them in advance to the next item).

III

There are, however, other possibilities. A site may actually be designed to accommodate a variety of movements, as Lord Perceval seems to have identified at Stowe; or, if designed with one particular movement in mind (because culturally expected), it allows itself to be visited with a different momentum and purpose (which may also be the consequence of changed cultural conditions). Whim, curiosity and personal initiative, which seem to direct the ramble, may also subvert a site visit where a more ritualistic visit was anticipated; equally, this may be brought about by a visitor's unfamiliarity with a place or with the cultural assumptions that govern its use.

Scudéry's *Promenade de Versailles* is an interesting case. Although Versailles was not planned as a site for ritual movement, it quickly became one during the 1660s, when predetermined forms of *bosquet* and *allée*, plus social conventions outside designers' control, to which however they responded, as well as the elaboration of a royal iconography (likewise not confined to the gardens), all combined to orchestrate how visitors would proceed through the grounds. Scudéry was a privileged exegete of this particular mode of visitation. Her *récit* tells how a group of courtiers promenade, talk, exchange reflections, and also

64 Detail of Etienne Allegrain, *Le bassin du Miroir et l'Ile Royale*, 1688, oil on canvas.

acknowledge other groups doing exactly the same – we see this imaged in several contemporary paintings (illus. 64). Visual descriptions draw on their own rhetorical repertoire to recount social and ideological assumptions that are clearly shared by all the French courtiers and include acknowledgement of 'the great qualities' of Louis XIV, the only begetter and the subject of Versailles.[21] The visit that she narrates does not propose a particular route, but it does make the experience of the gardens into a ritual of appreciation and understanding, both of the overall message and its local forms:

You can also see from this spot other parterres, other fountains, and to the left a nicely somber allée of pine trees, and a thousand different objects. . . . I will conduct you into a labyrinth of rustic berceaux with statues. . . . We made after that a hundred walks in these superb gardens . . .[22]

But among Scudéry's imaginary group is l'Etrangère, who is overwhelmed by the sheer variety and unintelligibility of garden items and whose presence effectively calls into question the other characters' mode of visitation, even though she (like the reader) is educated into the ritual as the visit proceeds. Another contemporary but in this case an 'insider', André Félibien, also chose to be baffled by the profusion of items,[23] but l'Etrangère's visit implies that an outsider left on her own and without the guidance of initiates would merely stroll through the profusion of scenes without any overall recognition of their individual or collective meanings.

Some later gardens seem to have allowed for these different responses, either through the resources of an original design or as a result of subsequent modifications of it. Alexander Pope's Twickenham garden combined a central, processional space with

65 Plan of Alexander Pope's garden at Twickenham, Middlesex, published by his gardener John Serle in 1748.

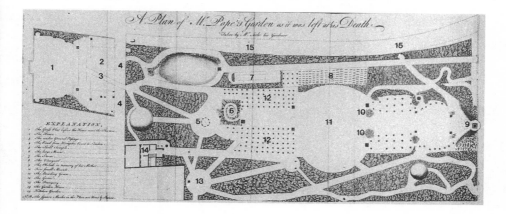

66 William Kent,
View in Pope's Garden,
1730s (?), pen and ink
with wash.

marginal areas through which small paths meandered (illus. 65).
The first led the visitor through what Horace Walpole described
as a procession: 'the passing through the gloom from the grotto
to the opening day', with these 'opening and closing shades'
leading finally to the cypresses backing an obelisk dedicated to
the memory of Pope's mother (Walpole called it a 'tomb', which
perhaps underlines his sense of ritual involved). One of Kent's
famous sketches of part of this central segment of Pope's garden
wittily characterizes this ritualistic contrivance with an apparatus
of temple, smoking altar and descending deities (illus. 66): the
temple was actually there, but the other elements represent
Kent's understanding of how the garden was to be received.
The lateral paths, in contrast, provided scope for strolling, perhaps
from urn to urn and with glimpses through the adjacent groves

into the central portion, before the visitor arrived obliquely at the maternal obelisk. Moreover, the famous grotto, to which Walpole refers, seems to have authorized both kinds of visitation within the same space. Contrived in what was effectively the basement of the villa, its rooms were surfaced with hundreds of emblems and encrusted geological specimens. After the poet's death, his gardener published a guide to the grotto that conducted the reader / visitor, as guides inevitably do, piece by piece, from room to room, all the while noting the source of each specimen; such a ritual may presumably, since the gardener adopts its format, have been something that Pope himself followed on occasions. But the rooms would also have allowed especially uninitiated visitors to stroll through without such a precise agenda, improvising and personalizing their responses to the ensemble.

Another contemporary garden, as already implied, also allowed different kinds of experience. Lord Burlington's Chiswick was eventually laid out with two emphatic *pattes d'oie* or goose-foot *allées*, their three arms aligned on specific buildings and their convergence also marked by some focal point; yet between these strong linear avenues were groves through which wriggled much more intimate paths. The open and social spaces were celebrated by painters whom Burlington commissioned to record public visitation: most notably Jacques Rigaud around 1734 emphasized the ritual or processional movement of considerable numbers of visitors through Chiswick (see illus. 34). So, too, did Pieter Andreas Rysbrack (painting probably in 1729 or 1730); but he also provided hints of alternative modes of visitation. Several paintings celebrate the Chiswick gardens as places where small groups would stroll, like those entering the Orange Tree Garden through a side opening in the surrounding hedge; since the formal spaces of Chiswick's layout did not essentially change, we may see the gardens in Rysbrack's imagery as being annexed for alternative kinds of exploration and movement.

67 Pieter Andreas
Rysbrack, detail of
*A View of the Avenue
Leading to the Bagnio,
Chiswick, c.* 1729–30.

Furthermore, in one exciting detail (illus. 67) he shows a lady stepping out of, or maybe into, one of the 'rambles' that lay within the tall hedges of the *pattes-d'oie*. Unfortunately and significantly, these were not parts of the gardens much recorded, although some of Kent's sketches reveal intimate moments and private corners of these gardens.[24]

Like Chiswick and his own Twickenham, Pope would have known another garden, Rousham in Oxfordshire, that has played a crucial role in understanding the history of garden design; but it offers some intriguing insight also into reception. Partly because it has never attracted visitors in large numbers, Rousham has never elicited a guidebook (plans are, however, provided for modern visitors), and therefore I doubt if any processional or ritual movement through its tight and intimate spaces was ever established. It has, to be sure, certain spaces more formally rendered and maybe susceptible to such visitation: the bowling green between the house and the river or the long elm walk terminated at one end by the statue of Apollo and at the other by an oblique view of the Praeneste Terrace. However, its insistent invitation is to stroll: at the end of the bowling green, for instance, the visitor must decide whether to follow the ha-ha around the paddock, descend sharply to the left and reach the theatre, or by turning down to the right reach the river, Classical seat and the pyramid. Strollers, in fact, have the chance of many different routes,[25] where the sight and the mind are constantly engaged by the surroundings. And this was how Kent's restructuring of the grounds in 1739 affirmed Rousham as a stroll garden in the contemporary taste for such a visitation.

Nonetheless, strolls through Rousham can well be ritualized. In the early 1750s its steward McClary wrote to its absentee owners to persuade them to spend more time there; he did so by narrating what he took to be their preferred route through the gardens.[26] It is as if his suasion can succeed only if he can remind them of a ritual now sadly unperformed and sunk into neglect because of the family's prolonged absence. Maybe there was a familial visitation of the gardens exactly as he describes it, or he was just trying to invent a ritual that he thought would please them; but not being himself a member of the family his account of the garden misses several nuances that its intimates would surely not have neglected – he fails to name Praeneste Terrace – and his attempt to ritualize the place seems gauche and facetious. What is intriguing, then, about McClary's letter is not that there was a fixed and predetermined route around Rousham, but that he invents one somewhat against the grain of its design.

Yet ritualization may take other forms. We have seen that Horace Walpole celebrated Pope's Twickenham garden by recalling a virtually processional movement through its 'little scenes'. In 1764 or thereabouts Walpole also visited Rousham and was reminded of the Emperor Julian and the territories where he consorted. Like Finlay making the same allusion in the public park at Luton (see above, p. 107), this appropriation seems to signal the attempt at some later moment to ritualize a site that otherwise and at other times and for other people is accessed less prescriptively. Walpole is in effect drawing Rousham into his mythologizing history of English garden design. The same kind of move that Walpole makes is fulfilled elsewhere simply by naming part of a landscape after famous or heroic figures: Pope's seat at Hagley; Kent's seat (very ruined) at Hackfall; Addison's Walk at Magdalen College, Oxford; Alfred's Tower on the ridge above Stourhead, or the same king's Hall at Cirencester; Shenstone's Priory at Enville. And anyone with a strong historical imagination and probably some sense of piety can invent a personalized processional route around the modern Rousham, through the sad remains of Pope's grotto, or in any historical site to which they are deeply attached or for which they have some particular affection. The interpretations of Jeffersonian designs at Monticello or Poplar Forest guide their visitors in ways that, on the one hand, are more or less subtly ritualized by the modern institutions that own and interpret them, but which, on the other, also rely on an individual's knowledge and willingness to be moved (in both senses) by the site.

IV

Narratives of use or reception intersect with narratives of design; these latter may be confirmed or challenged by the former. Clearly the Picturesque landscape has acquired a reputation for promoting a certain kind of movement: Camillo Sitte's late nineteenth-century proposals for town planning according to artistic principles recommends that 'A picturesque effect could be attained by following the natural path of a stroller's feet. Such a graceful curvilinear trajectory is observable in the villages and is an honour to imitate'.[27] But we also know, from detailed observations and analyses by F. Hamilton Hazlehurst, that pre-Picturesque gardens such as André Le Nôtre's Vaux-le-Vicomte or Dampierre only rendered their full potential to a moving observer who could be alert to the subtle optical tricks and metamorphoses of space and shape that had been built into the designs.[28] And modern accounts such as Hazlehurst's augment our current sense of Baroque design by returning us to more nuanced versions of an original reception process.

Physical changes to a site, which may be designed or the accidental result of decay and neglect, will result in different responses by visitors; so will cultural developments. Once Stowe eliminated its parterre and opened up the lawns on the south front towards the lake and the triumphal arch, movement into and through the grounds must have been modified, as the fresh disposition of spaces near the house prepared visitors in a different fashion for what lay ahead in the further parts of the garden. Sites that have not been altered and continue to exert their original hold upon visitors (the *sacri monti*, for example, for

Catholics) maintain their original invitations and are received in ways that have changed little since the seventeenth century. Whereas, since we do not presumably regard Louis xiv in the same light as did his contemporary subjects and paid mythologists, we respond to Versailles, even as historians, in different ways that ultimately effect how we talk about it now.

The *longue durée* of major landscape architectural sites suggests that designs are great in part because, like great works of music or theatre, they are hospitable in succeeding periods to many kinds of performance and reception, including those that come from different cultures than the one that designed them. So we should study the palimpsest of these successive responses as a means of understanding both the potential of the original design and of its continuing appeal. For this a taxonomy of movement proves particularly fruitful.

SEVEN

Moving Along in the Automobile

Speed is the queen of the modern world
FERNAND LÉGER

I

Many people still walk and explore gardens and landscapes on
foot; equally, some can still, as more privileged folk once did,
ride through them on horseback or drive along in carriages –
King Henry v even visited Kenilworth by barge. But there
are modern modes of travel that have revolutionized how we
experience landscapes – the railway, the motor car and the aero-
plane have changed the speed with which we are able or are
required to respond to our surroundings.[1] They have radically
effected the reception of landscape by requiring people to
respond more quickly, on the one hand, and by allowing
comparisons to be made with different and older speeds of
movement, on the other. They have also democratized landscape
experience both by transporting more people further from their
familiar home bases than ever before and by opening up more
territories to visitation.

The *New York Times* reported that when Václav Havel retired
after sixteen years as president of the Czech Republic he com-
pared his early travels across Europe to Britain in an old French
Simca sedan with his drive to Spain in 2003 in a Mercedes sports

utility vehicle: 'I thought we would see a lot', he was reported as saying, 'but we actually didn't see anything. We were traveling on highways and freeways and we were going through no cities, no villages, not even landscapes. All we saw were just bare roads'.[2] Havel's experience is shared by many, for whom, it seems, modern landscape architecture has largely ignored the opportunities of designing for the modern world of fast transport. To be sure, those highways are graded, their margins re-seeded and maybe replanted, their intersections often a dazzling sculptural swirl of curving concrete ramps with the interstices planted with new trees and green sward; but all that is essentially the world of the engineer (illus. 68). Railways (or railroads) have fared no better: again, some engineering feats have introduced into the landscape exciting new forms of viaduct, cutting and tunnel, while at the other extreme the gardenesque treatment especially of rural and suburban railway stations in Europe delights the alighting tourist who stops to explore the countryside or some *pater familias* returning from work every evening; there are even in Britain competitions for the most beautiful station landscapes.

68 'LANDSCAPING IN PROGRESS', California.

But essentially the modern highway and the railway line have escaped the attention of modern landscape architects, even though their profession came of age during the period when these new modern modes of travel were being elaborated, and they might have been expected to take up those particular challenges more extensively.

Not that there lacks some considerable literature on the landscape of roads, but its ambitions have been pragmatic and occasionally aesthetic, and its concerns little focused on what motorists themselves might derive from the experience of their travel other than safe and tolerable driving conditions. There is an exhilaration about much of the engineering forms developed for highway construction, a fascination with photography taken at high speeds, a somewhat elitist concern to ward off the strip-mall vernacular sprawl of suburban America or the billboards that punctuate rural highways, and in a volume such as *A View from the Road*[3] a real focus on drivers' reactions to existing highways through urban centres like Boston; the authors also attempt a graphic language to document visual sequence through built-up areas. This proves an interesting score card, along with its necessary verbal supplements, of the overwhelming barrage of sights that a driver might register, but an inventory that is merely descriptive and leaves little scope for discussion of what might be more plausible let alone stimulating experiences. It must be said that the resources of landscape architectural design are barely tapped; the traditions by which pedestrian visitors have been involved in their landscape experience rarely mentioned (passing references, notwithstanding, to approaches to a Japanese shrine or vignettes from Humphry Repton[4]) let alone extrapolated for these new conditions; much lamentation, after the fact, of the intrusive visual insertions of modern roadways into older cities and the consequent destruction of historical sightlines.

A distinguished landscape architect like Sylvia Crowe, publishing *The Landscape of Roads* in Britain in 1960, saw her topic as 'one of the most challenging landscape problems of today' (p. 12) and its essential solution as the proper relationship of new roads to their surroundings, just as an older network of rural connections and lanes had done. She canvasses various topics from policy, planning and design issues to structures, planting, parking and picnicking. The overall concern is on laying new highways into the land in such ways as will enhance both their own beauty and avoid damaging (if they cannot contribute to) that of the countryside. Here the role of the landscape architect *as designer* is frequently invoked, but, apart from the basic assumption that motorists will appreciate what is attractive in new engineering and re-landscaping, there is little concern for what those motorists might be led to experience. Design enjoys no afterlife except in road maintenance and clear directional signage.

There have been, of course, fascinating exceptions. In the 1860s the Parisian park of Buttes-Chaumont by Adolphe Alphand included, as a conspicuous part of its modern scenery, along with iron suspension bridges, concrete railings and false grottoes (see illus. 17 and 18), the suburban railway track that once took locomotives through the edge of the new park. In similar fashion during the 1850s the Türkenschanzpark in Vienna had incorporated the railway line that took hikers from the city out into the Semmering mountains a hundred kilometres away.[5] Yet both these examples are rather a case of landscapers taking advantage of railway lines than of their designing specifically for the new transportation. Thus, in another of his parks to the west of Paris, the Bois de Vincennes, Alphand welcomed the sight of already existing lines:

> two railways, that of Lyon and that of Orleans, enliven the landscape with the waving plumes of smoke from their locomotives. . . . And finally, as a backdrop to the view, one perceives the magnificent viaduct of the Mulhouse railway whose arches stand clearly against the blue sky.[6]

Some railway building has been able to take advantage of already existing scenery, without much disturbance of it: for example, from the last third of the nineteenth century the whole infrastructure of Swiss transportation from funiculars to cable cars took sublime advantage of the landscapes into which they were introduced, usually paying some careful attention to the insertion of these new machines into the increasingly touristical mountains. Equally, landscape architecture has occasionally acknowledged the new modes of transport and their destinations, but again without offering to invent or change land that lies along the route of rail or roadway. As early as the Türkenschanzpark, it was planned to 'announce' the final destination of its railway line in the Semmering mountains by representing aspects of that distant scenery (waterfalls, alpine plantings) within the suburban parkland; hikers were thus invited to prepare themselves for their destination by suggestions in the surroundings at their point of departure. This is also the device adopted by the designers of the much more recent Jardin Atlantique above the Gare Montparnasse in Paris.[7] Created upon a platform slung above the departure *quais* of the TGV (the fast trains that leave for the Atlantic coast), the public garden wittily re-creates a whole repertoire of seaside effects – boardwalks, 'waves' coming up the 'beach', caverns in the cliffs, seashore planting, weather stations, marine-blue tennis courts and children's nautical playground equipment (dolphins and galleons). The departing travellers can have their minds prepared for what they will see on arrival – a virtual seaside to put them in the right frame of mind to encounter the real one (alternatively, those who are not travelling may nonetheless imagine themselves already at that new location).

The reception of landscape by fast-moving travellers depends on a combination of circumstances: the speed at which a territory is traversed, which depends on such factors as a road's trajectory and gradient, the proximity and intrusions of surrounding land-scapes (urban, suburban or rural), the obligation or opportunity to modulate speed or even pause, and of course local speed limits. A brief, personal example of how experience of road travel is changed by the different speeds and the alternative routes that fast highways are forced to take will be useful.

For three years I lived and worked in the small Virginia village of Upperville, about 80 kilometres to the south-west of Washington, DC, to which city I would go by car several times a week (it was indeed the only means of access, at least until the point where I could have parked and taken the metro into the city). I had basically a choice of two routes. One took me up Route 50 and directly into the city in approximately 90 minutes. The other allowed me, after a brief initial spell on the same road, to take a detour of about 15 kilometres along country roads and then to join Interstate 66, along which I could reach Washington at greater speed. The different experiences provided by these two means of access to the city – indeed the sense that each time I set out I had a choice of what kind of experience I wanted or was in the mood for – suggest much about what J. B. Jackson, in a happy neologism, called *odology,* the science or study of road travel. It also reaffirms his argument that roads are themselves 'places'.[8]

While Interstate 166, once reached, would take me into the centre of Washington without stopping (no traffic lights, no filling stations, no intersections – though with frequent rush-hour congestion at the suburban exit and entrance ramps), Route 50, after a fairly straight run through farming and horse country, encountered many traffic-lighted intersections in small

towns, commercial sectors and suburban clusters. As a result
both of speed limits (80 km/h on Route 50, 106 km/h on the
Interstate) and of the character and lateral structures along the
side of each route, I had two very different experiences of landscape. Route 50 was a cocktail of American items and icons,
much of which I could grasp as a result of my slower speed,
frequent stops, and the proximity of the lateral sceneries to my
vision: at first there were farms, barns, small landing strips with
single engine planes parked under the trees like automobiles,
avenues leading off the road through portentous pillars towards
distant and not always visible mansions, small vernacular houses
at the roadside with their expressive flower gardens (illus. 69) or
a medley of parked cars and trucks alongside a graveyard of earlier
models; then, a sequence of small, distinct towns, followed by
the more predictable suburban realm of 'townhouses' (a curious

69 A house and
garden along Route
50 in northern
Virginia.

neologism in itself), shopping malls set back from the road with
their own parking, filling stations, churches and car-sale franchises.
It was above all a lived-in and worked landscape – people in the
fields, on the sidewalks, on porches of houses, always visible and
an intimate part of the changing landscape.

The Interstate by contrast offered a much broader panorama,
where people figured in miniature or not at all, with little for me
to observe in close-up along the margins and anyway flashing
past too quickly to register much detail. The dual carriageway
also took a somewhat winding route through the countryside
(illus. 70 – a complete contrast to the almost straight, workman-
like Route 50), with the result that the middle and far distances
became more important, always swinging gently back and forth
across the windscreen, beginning with the eastern side of the
Blue Ridge Mountains, where I joined the Interstate, across a
watershed crested with rocks thrusting up into the woodland,

to a fertile plain increasingly devoured by housing developments
(more 'townhouses') that were soon hidden behind noise barriers
that effectively led traffic through low-walled artificial canyons,
and finally across the open Potomac River and into the generous
spaces of federal Washington. In its own way, it was also a
prime American experience, emphasizing space and speed, the
nonchalance of endless and open roads, a wider-angled landscape generalized both by the absence of people and the relative
unimportance of local nuance. One route was the result of
incremental social and cultural growth over many years, with
no design intention or direction except perhaps in fragmentary
ways, but rich and eclectic in its randomness; in the other a
recent, calculated gesture was engineered with little concern for
anything but swift progress and minimal interaction between
motorists and their surroundings. (It should be noted that I am
not concerned to enter a debate about the 'good taste' of cultural landscapes like Route 50 versus the more 'aesthetic' and
sanitized throughways of Interstates;[9] what concerns this chapter
is the ways in which travellers may be involved more intensively
and profitably in the experience of their travels.)

III

These experiences suggest that there are in fact two modes of
experience for the traveller along fast, modern roads, modes
that a landscape architect might be called upon and be particularly qualified to address, since each requires a different agenda
from those followed by highway engineers. In one, motorists
must respond to vast stretches of territory as they fly by, often
for hours on end and with little apparent variation; the other has
to do with the need and opportunities for pausing, for rest and
relaxation stops during those speeding advances on an often
distant destination. (There is perhaps a third mode, somewhat

uneasily nestled between these two: the American parkway, in vogue when automobile speeds were much less than they now are, that sought to move travellers through either suburban or rural territory at a decent speed yet allow them the chance to appreciate its scenic character and shelter them from the 'bad taste' of urban sprawl – Rock Creek Parkway in the District of Columbia, the Merritt in Connecticut, or the Blue Ridge Parkway in Virginia.)[10]

Both kinds of reception – the speeding and the stationery – have been identified and addressed in some recent designs, conspicuous for their response to the exigencies, excitements and advantages of travel along highways (freeways, *autoroutes*, expressways, *Autobahnen*). An increasing body of built work in France is worthy of study for formal and environmental reasons, not least for the political initiatives from both the public and private sectors that sustain such work; but its main interest here is how deliberate and focused has been the designers' attention to the needs and experience of car drivers and their passengers.

There is an important connection between movement and pause, upon which highway travel offers some unusual perspectives. Henri Bergson wrote that 'we think of motion as if it were made of stillness, and when we look at it, we reconstruct it with the help of moments of stillness'.[11] Although some writers on landscape experience like Wotton, Watelet or Heely have in fact narrated their impressions of reception while on the move and been able to articulate motion *qua* motion, it is true that much discussion of movement seems focused on the pauses, the stationary interstices of onward momentum, by which that movement itself is measured. Highway travel, however, is almost entirely a matter of endless, forward motion, where stops constitute only a fraction of that experience; landscape architects who do address these issues have consequently to find some ways in which to cater as much for that onward momentum as for the more obvious rest areas. And the connections between these two elements of movement are therefore of increased importance.

The first mode of experience is the more difficult to address. At high speeds the eye of the driver if not of his passengers cannot be distracted by much busy detail on either side. It is the middle and far distances that lie in front of the vehicle that s/he can take in safely. Yet these inevitably lie outside the physical control of those responsible for the highway construction, being territory owned by other persons or entities. There are ways to overcome this limitation, one of which is to so engineer the direction of the highway so that landmarks – whether natural or man-made – present themselves clearly and safely and largely ahead of the moving vehicle. In the United States this is the means through which, by either deliberation, the exigencies of terrain or happenstance, some major highways introduce their travellers to the local territory. Driving up Interstate 189 from Massachusetts into Vermont, for example, along the western side of the Connecticut River, it is impossible not to be struck by what appear to be deliberate manoeuvres that bring the driver into appealing relations with the wooded and mountainous landscape; this functions at both the large-scale and with detailed textures, as the road variously crests a rise, runs along an elevated contour or is led through specially excavated canyons of granite. In France this attention to notable local features is also facilitated by large brown panels that announce nearby cultural monuments and districts in sufficient time for the occupants of the car to observe them even at a distance; these have the additional appeal of signalling different regions, lifting out of the homogenous territory as it streams past a variety of local events, products, buildings, activities. The invitation to detour and explore is of course always there, to be taken up if circumstances and curiosity allow.

But another way is to find the opportunity to direct vision by manipulating the surrounding landscape in ways that accommodate high-speed experience, perhaps by bringing into close proximity to the traveller strong, almost abstract versions of the surrounding terrain. This has been a device explored by Bernard Lassus, who has published some of his proposals and built work in *The Landscape Approach* (1998). Since his earlier experiments with vision and optical experience, Lassus has sought to involve viewers in what is viewed, leading them from visual (usually more distant) to tactile (close-up) experiences. In more recent work with the Ministry of Transport and the various private entities that own and control different segments of the French motorway system, he has expanded on some of those laboratory discoveries by exploring experiences of the path in different contexts and at various scales.

He sees the path or the highway as 'a plastic tracing *offered for view*, which hides in order to reappear according to the variations of the ground and what it supports'.[12] This can involve, in the work for Autoroute 85 (the Longué Interchange), a careful plotting of viewsheds vis-à-vis the actual route of the highway and the manipulation of adjacent elements of the terrain: massing of lateral woodland, for example, so that new vistas burst into focus, screens of new plantations to mask items or simply to steer the eye elsewhere, and that familiar French device of axial

71 Bernard Lassus, sketches of landscapes visible from a section of Autoroute 85.

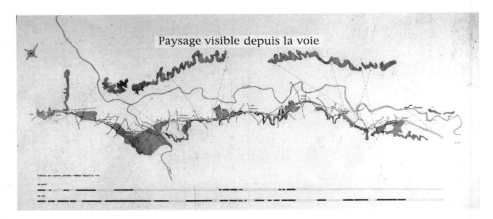

Paysage visible depuis la voie

"Le Grand Prince"

72 Bernard Lassus, design project for oblique views, including 'Terracing and Vegetalization', on Autoroute 85.

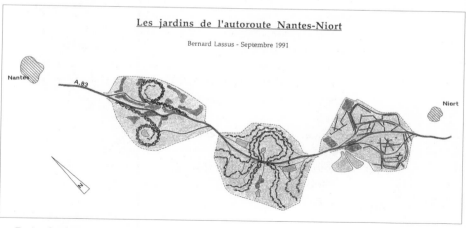

Les jardins de l'autoroute Nantes-Niort

Bernard Lassus - Septembre 1991

Nantes

A.83

Niort

73 Design for the 'Gardens of the Autoroute, Nantes–Niort'.

percées that lead the eye through to some more distant feature, house or spire (illus. 71 and 72). In another scheme for a segment of Autoroute 83 between Nantes and Niort the small-scale manipulation of features visible at large in the countryside – in this case hedges – is used to identify and characterize three rest areas (illus. 73); here the different organization of hedgerows in straight lines, meanders and rigorous circles both invites the motorist to register a dominant but perhaps otherwise unremarked element of the countryside, its hedges, by abstracting them at a more intense scales, and also encourages him or her to notice that rest areas are not homogenous.

IV

The other mode by which motorists experience landscape is of course when they are for a variety of reasons encouraged to stop, to buy more petrol, go to the toilet, get something to eat and drink, or just to rest or sleep for a while. In a country of essentially small distances, like England, these motorway rest areas are horribly utilitarian, with little desire to declare their locality – the main gesture in this direction is the display of some map of the surrounding countryside with a marker 'You Are Here'. On the American Interstate system there are no such areas on the highways themselves, so motorists are forced off to seek whatever facilities are desired, which notionally introduces them to some locality, but where the indications of place identity and character are either deliberately not emphasized because no design or even planning has guided the presentation of these locations, or because the generic franchises, gas stations or fast-food joints refuse all acknowledgement of local place.

Some of Lassus' work in France suggest alternative strategies. We have seen already along the A83 that rest areas could be given different schemes, although invoking at a most intense

dimanche 13 août 95
Br L. ⑨

scale just one item, the ubiquitous hedges of rural France. These configurations, impinging closely on the roadways, obviously alert drivers to the possible interests in stopping and in choosing where to stop, given the different treatment of each. That is the dramatic effect of another scheme for Crazannes on the Autoroute Saintes–Rochefort: suddenly the motorist finds his route closely bracketed by outcrops of rock, in fact ancient quarries discovered during motorway construction, excavated and remodelled for greater effect (illus. 74). They make a striking variation in the scenery, strange, even mysterious, as they flash past; but they also invite the motorist to turn off into the rest areas, about which panels back on the route have alerted him.

So Crazannes demonstrates that, given such visual emphasis on local features, motorists can be encouraged to stop and see what it was that pressed so suddenly and strangely on their immediate lateral vision. For travellers in both directions at Crazannes, Lassus designed rest areas where cars could park, children play and their families relax or picnic within circles freed of moving vehicles. Or, calling first at a visitors' centre, they can take more time and along paths and elevated belvederes explore

74 The quarries of Crazannes alongside the autoroute, drawn by Bernard Lassus.

the strange world of these ancient quarries, where a rare fern (*scolopendrium*) grows and where notices will tell of famous buildings around the world that used material from these old stone quarries.[13] What is so exciting about this project is that not only does it delay and entertain the long-distance motorist and make him aware of the richness and density of localities that otherwise he would speed through oblivious of their stories, but the local inhabitants too have demanded access to this place via a side road, so that they can also see for themselves the historical and botanical resources of their own backyard.

The autoroutes of Europe are now extensive and monotonous and empty of much interest, as President Havel noted ('not even landscapes'). Motorists can drive from Spain to Austria, from northern France to Sicily, without ever having to leave these thoroughfares. Apart from the considerable dangers posed by exhausted drivers who simply will not be bothered to linger in rest areas, because the pull of the ultimate destination marginalizes any interest in the route itself and because these stopping places are boringly utilitarian and unspecific, such travelling eliminates any understanding and appreciation of place. Crazannes suggests that it is possible for a landscape architecture to make memorable locations out of the functional gas and food stops through a detailed understanding of a given territory and its history, as well as to give to both visitors and local inhabitants a more interesting, even a more poetic, perspective on an otherwise anonymous place.

If Crazannes opens up (quite literally) the meaning and identity of an otherwise invisible rural site, another rest area, this time outside the city of Nîmes, reveals the rich history of a nearby urban conglomeration.[14] At the rest area of Nîmes-Caissargues the long haul from Italy to Spain may now be broken at a place where certain specific narratives of the locality can be read across the sloping site: there is the French reference to its Classical landscape architecture in the huge, tree-lined *allée*

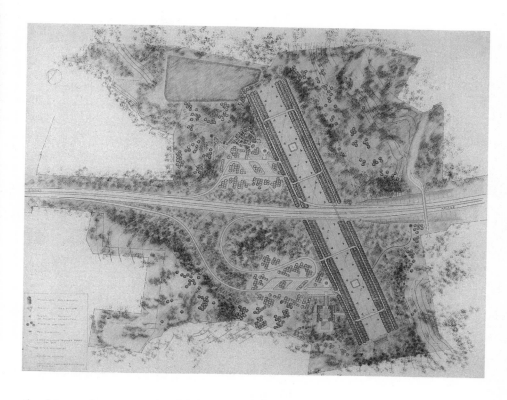

that bisects the autoroute and provides shade from the sun and
shelter from the winds of this Mediterranean site (illus. 75);
belvederes in the shape of the famous Tour Magne, one of the
famous monuments in Nîmes, enable visitors to look down
towards that city; but models of the Tour are also available
in the belvedere and a model of the ancient city, as well as a
museum dedicated to the Lady of Caissargues, were planned
for the site. In all, it is an intricate narrative of what Lassus calls
'Nîmeness', the identity and spirit of a place; now it attracts
passing trunk drivers as well as local inhabitants from Nîmes
itself. The pleasures and instruction offered by the site are
aimed at drawing visitors into a more informed if only passing

75 Plan for the
rest area at Nîmes-
Caissargues.

experience; clearly some will derive more enjoyment from it than others, although there seems to be something there for all tastes and needs. From the very start of the design process, it was understood by architect and clients alike that it is in its reception, its afterlife, that the rest area of Nîmes-Caissargues would have its best existence.

EIGHT

The Afterlife of Gardens and the Implied Visitor

Nobody 'will find preposterous that the past should be altered by
the present, as much as the present is directed by the past'.
  T. S. ELIOT, *The Sacred Wood*

si tel assemblage d'arbres, de montagnes, d'eaux et du maisons que
nous appelons un paysage est beau, ce n'est pas lui même, mais par
moi, par ma grace proper, par l'idée ou le sentiment que j'y attaché
  CHARLES BAUDELAIRE, 'Salon de 1845'

The subtle wonder of the ten thousand transformations
  ZHENG ZHEN, *Record of the Storied Pavilion of the Remote Heart*
  (late fourteenth century)

I

Claude-Henri Watelet's *Essai sur les jardins* draws a distinction
between the designing of a garden and the experience of it:

when an artist lays out a garden in the privacy of his own
study, uniformity and symmetry will result. Working on a
flat sheet of paper, he is inclined to render the surface of a
terrain uniform, when in reality it is uneven, to divide it into
lines that crisscross each other in a systematic fashion creating
repeated patterns, to trace straight allées, circular sections,

half-moons, or stars. What becomes of such a design when it is executed with all possible concern for the uniformity and order? The spectator surveys a part, guesses the rest, and feels only a mild desire to set out and explore . . . even if he were to undertake this tedious task, this walk that nothing encourages him to hasten or slow down, he would no doubt be like a man who moved his legs without going anywhere.[1]

Watelet no doubt caricatures for the purposes of his argument (he seems to assume a layout that by the 1770s would have been somewhat *retarditaire*, although the plan of his own Moulin Joli [see illus. 53] is not entirely free of the same 'patterns'); but his fundamental distinction is nonetheless clear — between, on the one hand, the design of a garden (he assumes its realization would not need to be compromised by the physical exigencies of the site) and the visitor's involvement (or lack thereof) with it, on the other.

The kind of distinction that Watelet draws might be illustrated by contrasting two Dutch paintings produced within five years of each other a century and more before Watelet was writing; they similarly reveal two different attitudes towards gardens and suggest that the distinction implied by Watelet was not unique to the Picturesque movement and its tendentious arguments. One, a personification of *Arithmetica* (illus. 76), draws our attention to the plan that the 'designer' holds up and which attests to his skill in its geometrical realization on paper. The other depicts an extensive family group on a garden terrace (illus. 77), where some members gesture over the garden that lies below, some are already starting their descent into it, and others can be glimpsed already strolling along its paths below; of course, there is no clear indication that the family's garden would be like that depicted on the designer's sheet; but given the period and culture it is likely to have been regular (or, as we too easily say, 'formal', despite the informality of its use that the painter shows).

76 Laurent de la Hyre, *Arithmetica*, *c.* 1650, oil on canvas.

77 Jacob van Oost, *A Bourgeois Family in their Garden*, 1645, oil on canvas.

So here we have images of two very difficult attitudes to
gardens – one drawing attention to the design, along with the
arithmetic skills needed by the designer to produce it; the other
to the various responses and experiences that a group of even
the most like-minded or socially coherent persons would have
of what must be a regular garden. Later writing would often blur
these two attitudes towards garden art. A few years after Watelet's
book, the German garden writer Hirschfeld (who relied on
Watelet's essay for his own volumes) seems to merge the two
perspectives in such a way that it is difficult to separate his
commentary on design from the proposed experience of its
different strategies:

> A park or very large garden requires a landscape of many
> different regions: valleys, hills, hollows, mountains, gentle
> slopes, and precipitous inclines, everything richly alternating.
> Where the ground offers such variety, vistas proliferate of
> themselves; it is one thing from the heights, another from the
> depths . . . Scenes disappear and reappear; new ones envelop
> the old; locales continually change. You climb, and the horizon
> expands on all sides; you see regions subside and fade away
> as you go higher; the blue dome of the sky stretches out to
> immensity and at its edge the light of the day pales in the
> hazy distance; amazement and admiration fill the soul.
> Gentler emotions take their place as you descend again to
> lower elevations. The sky itself seems to shrink back; at least
> part of its loveliness retreats behind the ascending land;
> slopes lead to meadows, woodlands, lakes.[2]

The 'you' of this passage is ambiguous. It is at once the visitor,
the person experiencing a landscape, and the controlling genius
of either the designer or the place itself. The passage begins
by assuming the perspective of the latter, commenting on the
elements that make up a successful design, and slides as the

paragraph proceeds into responding to the site as would a visitor in that parkland. The viewing subject and the object that s/he views become subtly intertwined.[3] We might, however, note that Hirschfeld is somewhat ambiguous as to the status of this ideal scenery: it could be the result of fortuitous yet fortunate topographical accidents, or the product of carefully designed intervention by remoulding a found territory into a superb parkscape. Yet, since he was well acquainted with Alexander Pope's famous passage that urges the designer to 'consult the genius of the place in all', a passage that effectively and strategically blurs the agency of good design,[4] Hirschfeld's passage may also be read as celebrating the successful conjunction of various design factors and the consequent ambiguity, too, of visitors' experience in such a parkland.

II

In the light both of these three pieces of evidence – Watelet's distinction, the analogous Dutch paintings from a century before him, and Hirschfeld's merger of the dual perspectives of designer and receptor – and of the various sites and texts that have been considered in the preceding essays, it is now worth trying to draw some conclusions about the afterlife of gardens. There are two main directions in which such considerations could lead: one is historiographical, and concerns how we might tell or modify the story of garden design from the point of view of its reception; the other looks forwards rather than backwards and asks to what extent an interest in garden reception might effect the ongoing practice of design and its analysis. The second, however, would need to rely on some acquaintance with historical records and methods if it is to establish some useful procedures of its own. Both concerns may find the idea of an implied or virtual visitor a useful concept by which to

guide their thinking. In the historical examples this virtual visitor
can usually be constructed from a variety of given, actual
materials, whereas for contemporary design we would need
often to project and invent such virtual visitation. As a consequence of this shared interest in virtual visitors, however,
both historical and design concerns may also find their interests
coincide more than is generally allowed by practitioners of
landscape architecture.

III

It is surely clear that as historical sites extend their lives into
later periods with changed cultural conditions, the original
configuration and its meanings are 'modified in the guts of the
living' (to recall Auden's celebration of the afterlife of Yeats's
poetry). The issue, then, is how we allow those modifications
into our historical readings of sites as well as – where relevant
– into our physical reformulations of those that continue to
exist but that, given the inherent transience of garden art, need
preservation or conservation.

A major issue that can be addressed via reception study is
the vexed question of meaning in landscape architecture; a
historical perspective here will elucidate the discussions of
meaning in contemporary design. In the first chapter, parallels
with literary reception were canvassed, and they suggested that
all reception in whatever medium was a 'dynamic happening',
in which there were no finite or inherent meanings but only
those received or constructed by subsequent 'readers'. But
one fundamental difference between designed landscapes and
literary texts is that the latter employ a system of signs in
structured and unfolding sentences, whereas the former rely
on 'embedded figures'[5] that permit different discoveries and
orderings, which result from their spatial disposition and how

those spaces are encountered. Some very special dynamics of meaning are therefore at work in landscape architecture.

Some gardens obviously provide more triggers and prompts than others and are even more deliberate with how the installations will promote readability – the Labyrinth at Versailles, for example, with its statues and engraved verses (illus. 78), Finlay's prosopopeiac insertions in both public and private locations, Stowe's anthology of temples and sculpture, are all sites where their very design insists on some dynamic interchange between them and their visitors. Furthermore, visitors at certain times have been more attuned to the need to read those figures and also to find some coherent way to connect in some fashion – as narrative, moral injunction, philosophical reflection – the isolated and maybe seemingly random items along their garden route; this expectation could take either the form of anticipating and then confirming some meaning (Scudéry's courtiers at Versailles) or discovering a meaning wholly unexpected in that particular place (Watelet's implied visitor or Gilpin's character Polython in dialogue at Stowe). At other periods, and notably in contemporary work, there is little expectation by visitors that some deliberate and even fairly complex interchange is expected of them, and puzzlement can occur when they are faced with materials that do seem to require such an exchange and yet are obscure or gnomic. When such an expectation is met, however, two kinds of reception may occur. If the meanings discovered or confirmed partake of what has been termed the 'natural attitude',[6] that is to say deriving from matters taken for granted in the experience of daily living, their reaffirmation in a designed site gives the meanings, I believe, a special resonance because of that very special situation. Alternatively, if the meanings are unfamiliar, then their discovery in a place that is deemed exceptional in some way, as *ipso facto* any designed site can be, further redounds to the quality of that site, contributing to its status as what the French term a *haut lieu* (a special place, not a matter of elevation).[7]

78 Jean Cotelle,
L'Entrée du Labyrinthe,
1693, oil on canvas.

But we have also seen that there came a point during the
Picturesque phase of gardening when the visitor chose or was
encouraged to invest his or her own meanings in sites rather
than feel constrained to respond to figures already 'embedded',
a situation that obviously can pertain today whether or not the

visitor's responsibilities and resources are in question as with some late eighteenth-century commentators. This may happen with a site deliberately un-programmed, without signs to be read – as would be particularly the case on un-designed sites – or it may transpire, against the grain of such inserted signs, when the visitor goes his own way in either route or response or both.

We do need, then, to draw adequate distinctions between visitors and their responses if we are to make profitable use of the latter. There are those who bring a full repertoire of knowledge to their visit, who display greater resources of imagination and memory, and we tend to accord these more authority when we want to know what a garden meant at a certain period: their number would include family members in the Stowe circle, Watelet's friends, or Louis XIV's courtiers who would not wish to lag behind in careful appreciation of the royal efforts. We also tend to credit those who spend more time on a site or visit it on more than one occasion, or show themselves to be experienced as garden visitors (John Evelyn springs to mind as somebody whose dedication to gardenist matters made him a valuable observer; so too, Horace Walpole, though here we have also to take more into account some strongly tendentious assumptions with which he set out his opinions on English landscaping[8]). However, it seems clear from the survey in chapter Five of early responses by visitors to Stowe that even the casual, hurried or inexperienced visitor can also afford us undeniable insights that cannot be gainsaid, especially if they seem to go against the grain of conventional design narratives.

There is also the problem of confusion between materials that will document reception and those that are used to disclose a site's design history along with original or intended meanings. Sometimes available forms of documentation will have made abundantly clear to visitors what a designer's intentions were, so that we may safely assume there is an identity between intention and reception: there were and are, for instance, 'authorized' guidebooks or interpretative visits that direct the attention of visitors to an intended meaning or narrative; these tend to channel responses along established and preordained lines. It is not, however, always clear that visitors either then or now will have access to the same range of materials as do the historians, bolstered by research and blessed with hindsight about such sources. Even when we can identify clearly established 'programmes' of iconography in a Renaissance garden, say, or a modern designer has spelt out his intentions,[9] it has still to be asked whether the visitor will know them. Furthermore, as has been noted in the first chapter, too often receptions of sites are collapsed or folded into narratives of design creation and implementation, which confuses a valuable distinction between intention and reception and consequently marginalizes a profitable alternative perspective that sees the site through the imaginations and the experience of those who cannot have known anything of the site's original programme and implementation. In fact, many historical sites have to be approached by extrapolating from a variety of sources, not all of which will have 'authorial' value; above all, the intentional fallacy – the notion that a designer's intentions explain results and moreover that those supposed results will be experienced by subsequent visitors as the original designers would themselves have anticipated – is put rigorously but dangerously to work

The case of Stourhead, in Wiltshire (illus. 79), allows a clear view of these possibilities and confusions. There have been a cluster of interpretations of this wonderful landscape garden, each of which builds hugely upon a slender body of evidence.[10] This evidence includes, most obviously, the various buildings, which have names and, in two cases, inscriptions (both from Virgil), the happy coincidence that a painting by Claude Lorraine in the house, *Coastal View of Delos with Aeneas*, approximates to the first vista that greets a modern visitor to the garden, and a few remarks in letters by or to Stourhead's owner, the banker Henry Hoare, who had the major role in the design of his own

grounds. What is fascinating about this critical literature is that it directs its considerable energies to establishing what the gardens meant to Hoare himself. Putting aside for the moment the whole question of the intentional fallacy – in this case: first, did Hoare's intentions get actually and clearly reified in the grounds as they were worked on over several decades? Second, what real evidence is there that those intentions were clearly read by visitors if they were so realized in the finished design? – the Stourhead literature can claim, in fact, little direct evidence of Hoare's intentions. As a result, it widens its focus and draws on a variety of cultural contexts that are presented as filling out, as fulfilling, the meagre materials about an 'authorial' meaning. This tactic necessitates the projection or 'invention' of an ideal or what here has been termed a virtual visitor, although in fact no actual ones are cited and the construction of the virtual visitor is thus left problematic and undefined.

79 A view in the gardens at Stourhead, showing the medieval cross brought from Bristol next to the parish church.

Thus two isolated quotations from Virgil's *Aeneid*, engraved respectively on the Temple of Flora / Ceres and above the original entrance to the Grotto, authorize, along with the Claudean subject-matter of the painting in Hoare's collection which is elevated into a major 'source' for the formal organization of the site, the construction of a whole narrative for the garden visit that parallels Virgil's story of Aeneas' escape from Troy, his adventures along the way including a descent to the underworld (i.e., the Grotto) and the eventual founding of Rome. To sustain this narrative parallel with the Latin epic poem, other elements of the garden are urged into complicity – the river god in the Grotto becomes Father Tiber who greets Aeneas, the Hercules statue in the Pantheon stands in for the city of Rome where he was worshipped; at the same time certain other elements – a sleeping nymph in the Grotto, the Market Cross, Alfred's Tower on a ridge beyond the gardens, and even later additions like a Gothick Cottage – are ignored. Then upon the foundation, already shaky, of this Virgilian parallel is raised a Christian version, since Aeneas's travels had been interpreted as 'a parable of the Christian soul's journey through life' which culminated in celestial wisdom (the Temple of Apollo on its ridge!). And so on.

Now the point here is not the 'looms of fantasy' at which critics have woven their rhetoric: Malcolm Kelsall did a fine scholarly job of putting the historical design of the gardens in a more nuanced cultural perspective. It is rather that the cultural context on which every one of these writers relies was a wide one, and it seems strange to opt for some parts and not others. The collective mental habits of mid-century visitors could have included some of the very elements that Kelsall finds preposterous in other explanations of Stourhead – a good eighteenth-century knowledge of Virgil, a fascination with typological histories that would make parallels between modern London and ancient Rome or Troy, even a wish to Christianize the classics – just as much as those strands that Kelsall feels crucial, namely a contemporary concern to honour local Saxon lore and English liberties – King Alfred and his Gothick tower – as an indigenous tradition to match and blend with that of Classical Roman. All of the above were habits of mind that visitors might have brought to their visit, even if we can be assured (which in the final resort we cannot) that some of them were not entertained by Hoare. Further it must be obvious that shared, general attitudes towards English history already formed outside the gardens and prior to any visitation of them are as likely to have directed visitors' responses as minutiae of specific knowledge, such as what paintings hung in the mansion or what references to Avernus Hoare had made jokingly in a letter.

Recently, yet another reading of the garden,[11] which depends now upon foregrounding the former Gothic market cross that was brought by Hoare from the mercantile city of Bristol and which visitors also pass as they first enter the grounds, helps to put into perspective some of the very tricky issues of meaning and the assumptions and sleights of hand that we use to identify and establish them. We prefer to pin down an original meaning, an authorized version of the site that is intricately tied to its design programme, although in practice we pick and choose among the original features of the site in proposing one, and when – as the very zany eclecticism of modern analyses shows – a whole other range of possible receptions can be shown to exist. None of Stourhead's critics invokes the reactions of actual visitors from any period at all, doubtless because few are recorded or, if they are, few help to address matters of original meaning, which is the explicit or implicit motive of their analyses. Yet what is most intriguing is that these same critics do rely precisely on specific receptions of the literary texts that are in question as part of their argument, while invoking only in the vaguest, uncritical terms a supposed eighteenth-century visitor – 'any educated visitor of the age'[12] – who is nothing in fact but a surrogate for their cluster of assumptions.

Stourhead comes to exist, it seems, in contested claims for meanings that can be shown to have been embedded in the original design by Henry Hoare on the basis of some tendentious reading of the cultural context. No analysis offers itself as a non- or a-historical reading of the site; none is presented, either, as the modification of Stourhead in the guts of the living. Even though its physical fabric has undergone many changes in 250 years (give and take all those rhododendra, for example!), it is assumed that origin meanings (whatever they are deemed to be) rule current reception. Although one has to have read this quite extensive literature to realize that a garden like Stourhead can elicit an astonishing range of meanings, a modern visitor without that knowledge gets little sense of the issues of interpretation and reception. Though it is judiciously presented and eschews a rigidly argued or structured scenario, the National Trust guide-books — Kenneth Woodbridge's revised edition, in particular, as Kelsall acknowledges — continue to shape a modern visitor's reception by steering it along respectable *historical* lines; the modern visitor is still asked to see the gardens as having one meaning or explanation or 'version' that derives from its original owner and creator.

Some preliminary distinctions therefore seem to be called for between interpretations, receptions, of gardens that have historical authority and those that respond beyond the evidence that their reception was either intended or available at a given time. So we can identify different interpretations: those that are grounded in a familiarity with the patron's and / or designer's documented intentions, but may or may not adduce evidence that such intentions were perceived by visitors; those again that draw with some confidence on a contemporary cultural mentality within which it seems plausible to see the original design developing, even though no evidence of that immediate connection is available and even though that cultural mentality is generalized beyond the contributions of any individual visitors; and those that float free of such evidence yet still respond with some imagination and insight. It is with these latter kinds of response that historians have difficulties, as Kelsall's essay on Stourhead makes patently clear. Yet it is not so clear that some of the discredited receptions are not plausible responses from a historical point of view, since many do indeed have support from cultural history; but even those that do not have that support, have, in fact, responded with an instinct for narrative cohesion, which suggests in itself an issue for receptions of garden and landscape design.

The richness of sites like Stourhead lies precisely in their ability to provoke and promote a wider sea of emotions, ideas, stories than was ever anticipated by Henry Hoare and his immediate family in the first instance or by the National Trust nowadays. So we must give some credence and support to the argument that over the *longue durée* of its existence a great design can stimulate a whole cluster of meanings that were not intended or envisaged for the original designs. This will disturb the historians, but those who profess to understand and revere landscape architecture should welcome the opportunities that allow a rich residue of meanings to accrue beyond the moment and the intention of a site's design. This surely has significance for contemporary design where historians have not yet exercised their forensic skills.

But there is another aspect of reception and its contribution to understanding the meanings of landscape architecture; this returns us to the unique quality of a designed landscape as a 'text', subject to kinds of reception that distinguish it categorically from discursive writings. Namely that the 'signs' that visitors interpret in their visitations of gardens have a reality, an existence, independent of their signage: the whole haptic, sensual experience of landscapes, their organic, material effects, the changes of light, the intricacies of texture, times of day and of season are NOT like the words on a page, even though they may be 'translated' into words by some garden writers. Sir George Sitwell in his essay *On the Making of Gardens*[13] notes that Italian

Renaissance gardens provoke an 'impression which it is difficult to analyse, to which no words can do justice'; he nevertheless provides fine examples of this verbalizing of the non-discursive elements of garden art, as this passage on the Villa d'Este as he knew it:

> Deep drifts of withered leaves have gathered on the stairways, the fountain basins are overgrown with maiden-hair or choked with water-weeds, the empty niches draped with velvety moss or tapestried creepers. Descending by weed-grown stair and crumbling balustrade, one reaches a gloomy alley where a hundred fountains gust into a trough beneath a line of mouldering reliefs. At the further end of the terrace, falling in great cascades like the folds of a Naiad's robe or the flash of a silver sword, the river [Aniene] leaps into the garden, to four great pools of troubled water, a jewelled belt which quivers in the sunlight with a mysterious, an amazing blue. Such is the garden in the sober daylight, but what it may be in the summer nights, when the breath of the ivy comes and goes in waves of drowsy perfume, and great white moths are fluttering about the fountains, and in the ilex arbours and gloomy alcoves there are strange mutterings, and deep-drawn sighs, and whispering voices, and flashes of ghostly white, I do not dare to say.

Words may of course have a sensual quality and thus a role to play in conveying an overall literary meaning, but rarely do they have an independent role, a reality that exists before and beyond how we interpret them and the story they convey. By contrast, a garden's various phenomena do impinge on a visitor independently of any meanings or stories he or she draws from his experience of the site. Sitwell's may seem 'dated' prose, too redolent of the *fin de siècle* (though he was writing later), but it does manage to suggest a range of haptic experience that is an ineluctable

aspect of most people's experience in a garden like the Villa
d'Este, even if other people might choose to express it differently.
And we can see this at work in some crucial instances already
discussed – Wotton responding to some incomparable Italian
site, Temple at Moor Park. Of course it is much more palpable
when the sites in question have little or no conventional iconography (illus. 80): the designs of Gertrude Jekyll or William
Robinson, the management of woodlands at Winterthur,
Delaware, or the designs of Roberto Burle Marx, who plays
infinitely and resourcefully with the materials at his disposal.[14]
Neither is this a matter solely of aesthetics, a much neglected
(and feared) issue in contemporary landscape architectural discussions; nor a result solely of horticultural expertise. While it
may certainly involve planting expertise and attitudes to and
ideas of beauty in design, the haptic reality of gardens tran-
scends both. As a crucial aspect of our experience, it contributes
at least in equal measure with more explicitly read and discursive
signs to the total 'meaning' of a garden. When some visitors to
Stowe contrasted the immense landscape of woodlands through
which they journeyed to reach the gardens with the different

alleys and walks within which they later found themselves, they are implicitly responding to the feel, texture and affective resources of the immediate site; that aspect of their reception is every bit as crucial to the whole as their adjudication of meanings in temples and sculptures. By contrast, none of the discussions of meaning at Stourhead addresses directly its haptic qualities – even though 'valings and mountings' (as Wotton said) become an active ingredient in reception of those meanings that invoke descents into the underworld or ascents into the realm of Apollo; nor do the substantial changes in the physical shape and feel of its plantations over the years play any role in defining meanings, yet it is surely improbable that they have no effect at all upon how a visitor reacts.

IV

The virtual visitor may be a useful device by which to accommodate all the various categories and modes of response that have been outlined here. In literary reception s/he is composed not of actual readings but of possible readings in a given situation. In landscape architecture we might sketch his profile from collections of actual readings of the site at all stages of its existence, especially from the implied responses of 'non-vocal' receptions – visual imagery of all sorts, especially where these seem particularly sensitive, like photography, to the haptic potentialities just discussed, and even from what we must term fictional accounts (including some 'scholarly' perspectives that fail on more conventional grounds of documentation!); many of these, while unprovable by the rules of historical evidence, capture and put into circulation an authentic sense of a garden.

The range of these materials that go to constitute a virtual visitor has also a temporal aspect that is separate from some historical perspective. That is to say that the reception of a site after its perceived or acknowledged heyday effects changes in how we view its original 'moment'; we view its origins in the light, often, of its latterday existence, or even disappearance. This is T. S. Eliot's point, quoted at the head of this chapter, on allowing the past to be altered by our present; or the late fourteenth-century Chinese sage who expressed his wonderment at the many transformations to which a place might be subject. In practice, of course, landscape architecture is constituted less of moments than by more or less *longues durées*, which in themselves complicate the transformation of the 'past' by the 'present': we cannot date 'Stowe'; what we name as Stowe is a site that evolved and continues to evolve decade after decade, and our response to it is premised on our unconscious acknowledgement that it has evolved into what we experience now. Even Versailles, for which we might try to argue for a more or less 'stable' moment of design during Louis xiv's reign, underwent a whole series of elaborate modifications and re-designs during his lifetime that effectively make nonsense of such an attempt. Yet in both cases later views of the site augment or transform how we might be led to see a moment during its earlier stages, somehow deemed more authentic. Such an 'authentic' moment can sometimes be established as a point of time in the design evolution or even realization on the ground for some gardens that were completed quickly – Carmontelle's Jardin Monceau was fairly rapidly constructed and might allow for such a convenient fiction. But even there its partial remodelling as a public park during the Haussmannization of Paris in the 1860s will determine how its original moment is now viewed, especially if we seek to 'read' what was once more extensively there as an elite private garden in the light of the fragments that remain in the public domain.

The concept of a virtual visitor will contribute variously to garden study. It will provide case studies of receptions over time at different cultural moments; this will demonstrate the kinds of response along with the kinds of control that elicited such responses; by this is meant that different responses will be produced and shaped both by physical changes on site and by different states of mind that each age will manifest irrespective of what design changes have been effected. This virtual visitation will also hopefully guide a more thoughtful modern attention to the role of reception in design (more of that below). It must also inevitably steer historical preservation or conservation.

Here there are several options. Of course, it may be used to document and argue for restoration of a historical site to one given period, although in so doing it is likely to highlight the innumerable 'irrelevant' aspects that have to be discarded or rejected in concentrating on one particular historical moment. More challengingly, evidence from the virtual visitor argues for the creation of a palimpsest where all stages or eras of a site can be appreciated; and each such 'moment' will bring its own cultural context and assumptions that need interpretation. For the elaboration of some implied visitor, either for a specific site or more generally for a given period, makes abundantly clear that any visitation depends on its own fabric of assumptions and beliefs, its own mentality, and that we ourselves cannot respond wholly objectively to a historical moment, since like any virtual visitation our own presuppositions and ideas have also gone into describing that historical moment. We touch here on the role of reception in any design, whether it is a design that tries to restore to a site its given historical parameters or a new one that re-makes or invents a site afresh.

V

Of course, many designers will have considered how their work will be experienced or used, even if their considerations are not always discernible in the historical record. Sometimes reception is programmed: one might instance any number of gardens

where inscriptions are meant to 'speak' to the passing visitor,
or where vistas are invented and presented to the eye, or where
paths direct visitation in ways that effect a particular experience
of the site – it would be hard to imagine an experience of
Versailles that does not place its visitors first on the terrace of
the château and stretch their sight down the terraces, across the
bosquets of the *petit parc*, then over the immense pools of water
to rest eventually on the empty space between the 'pillars of
Hercules', the twin trees that mark the western horizon (illus. 81).
And all that, it is worth emphasizing yet again, is preliminary to
and independent of the reception of iconographic meaning.

There are modern designers, too, clearly impelled in their
designs by how their work will be used and received.[15] In the last
chapter it was shown how eager was Bernard Lassus to capture
the attention and interest of long-distance motorists either as
they sped along the *autoroutes* or whenever they could be tempted
to stop and consider the specific yet apparently unmeaningful
location where they then found themselves. The American
designer Lawrence Halprin has also worked for decades to ensure

that his designs are both responsive to anticipated human use and are designed so as to allow a richer repertoire of response beyond what might be anticipated. His early work, *The RSVP Cycles: Creative Processes in the Human Environment* (1969), formulated a concept of design that has continued to guide all his work: Resources were the physical and human materials available, Scores described and plotted the process leading to the performance, the coinage Valuaction then analysed the results and selections of design decisions, and finally Performance 'is the resultant of the scores and is the 'style' of the process'; the conjunction of these terms was RSVP, meaning, of course, 'respond', although he is quick to point out that the fourfold system is not bound by that linguistic sequence and can take 'any other combination'.[16] It is an elaborate and in fact very spiritual rhetoric, clearly a means by which he was best able to clarify and articulate his artistic vision of designing for the 'interface' of humans and nature (Halprin invokes, if obliquely, Jung's 'compass of the psyche'). More immediately telling, though, is his insistence on choreography, for which he draws inspiration from his wife, who is a dancer. He writes of how their work seeks the 'root-source of human needs and desires' and through its physical resources – the forms, shapes and spaces of designed sites in his case, or the forms, arenas and dancers in hers – draws out rich responses. Hence his fascination with levels, ramps, stairs, connections, those spaces where what Wotton had called 'mountings and valings' will choreograph visitors' experience and help them 'perform' the site (illus. 82). This is a design philosophy and process that anticipate the creative collaboration of subject and object; by no means unwilling to propose and implement a design, for Halprin it is in the afterlife of that place that design is fulfilled.

There arise problems, however, in anticipating or relying on visitor response, and this is where a more rigorous understanding of historical receptions may assist the contemporary designer. Michel Conan has identified three kinds of response and their

manipulation that are premised largely on historical record; yet
it will be possible to suggest ways in which they may be reconfig-
ured to fulfil a contemporary designer's needs in this matter.[17]

There is, first and most obviously, the personal response –
an appeal that design students endlessly make, with the corollary
that if every person's response is different and as good as any
other, design cannot possibly address any of them (and so, the
individual designer falls back on his or her own solipsist repertoire, despite the fact that the built work is beyond their control
and will be modified in the guts of others' experience). One
answer to the insistence on there being a too-bewildering range
of personal responses for the designer to consider them is that
interpretation in its various forms – journalistic essays, guided
visits, printed guidebooks or audio-cassettes, all of which are
familiar to American tourists – can shape many individual
responses into one shared experience. But the provision of

82 Skyline Park,
Denver, Colorado,
designed by Lawrence
Halprin (now
destroyed).

such guides and instruction tends to be available only with well-established sites that attract a considerable flow of visitors.

The second of Conan's observations is that individual responses are indeed and necessarily formed by a given culture (this in fact parallels Halprin's diagram of two conjoined cycles, that of the individual and community[18]). Conan asks us to see 'experience as a mental state that plays on widely shared cultural contexts to frame a reflection on a string of bodily encounters with nature'; he borrows from phenomenology the term 'inter-worlds' or 'concrete intersubjectivities' to describe the recourse of one person's ideas and responses to such cultural systems as language, social roles and institutions.[19] This is clearly an area where contemporary designs can learn most readily, notwithstanding their frequent appeal to the multiplicity of personal positions. Yet the popular mantra of community design, whereby members of communities that would be most impacted by a site's (re)development are consulted by designers as part of a process to establish programme and even the physical outlines of the project, does not tap sufficiently into those cultural 'inter-worlds'; its empiricism and its often sentimental deference to a democratic process cannot guarantee the results that a more researched and conceptualized understanding of cultural forms can elicit. Here is surely where an adequate understanding of historical reception in landscape architecture can reveal how visitation of sites betrays the deep resources of both cultural communities and their fractures; not that we design nowadays for a cultural mentality that is outmoded, but we design with a more strenuous and nuanced understanding of how individuals draw their own ideas and concerns from a cultural matrix. The model of the anthropologist is exemplary here.[20]

The third stategy that Conan elaborates is one where experience itself can contribute to cultural change. Design can in this instance actually highlight 'the role of reception in the dissemination of a new aesthetics and the role of artistic creation in their invention'. This idea has some very interesting historical evidence to support it, although Conan himself moves in a rather different direction. He quotes Wolfgang Iser, already invoked in my first chapter as the central theorist of literary reception, to the effect that visitors / consumers of landscape architecture can be predisposed to 'a very specific kind of reception by announcements, covert and overt signals, familiar characteristics or implicit allusions'. One issue here is that such devices are more feasible and expected in literature than they are in landscape designs, and, as Conan has also noted himself, the former do not function with the same discursive logic as happens in landscape architecture; perhaps when landscape designs use inscriptions and other explicit signs, such direction of visitors is possible and can be called into play. But beyond a very literal and primarily discursive signage, landscape architecture is not able to be so explicit about its intentions and the need for visitors to read that signage.

However, there is one fascinating aspect of how experience plays into and upon cultural change. Put simply, it is that experience in gardens having often been against the grain of their design, at least as that is usually narrated, or, at the very least, having significantly augmented by an enlarged and expanded reception the original possibilities of the site, that experience has in its turn actually *directed* the next phases of design. *New design is driven by receptions of previous examples*, and we need a history that would explore that unexpected phenomenon in depth. Some elements of such a new narrative have emerged during these essays. Many eighteenth-century visitors to Stowe, for instance, responded to the site in ways that seem to put them 'ahead' of what the historical narrative usually identifies as a given stylistic moment in the evolution of the grounds. Watelet's essay on his own Moulin Joli, written as a letter to a friend, also communicates a very different impression of the site than does the surviving plan; even if we must admit that he was writing sometime after the garden was laid out and after the plan was drawn up and that he may well be expressing a change of opinion about how he responded to its formal layout, it is equally clear that his expectations and understanding of the site when he wrote in 1774 have overtaken the actual design. The evolution of much landscape design after Watelet suggests that in some fashion the instincts of his reception would later find more appropriate and answering forms.

There would seem to be a fundamental impact of reception on succeeding developments in design on many occasions.[21] To chart this is a challenge, but one that may well produce a somewhat different narrative of design history. We are accustomed, for example, to track the stylistic progress of so-called Mannerist garden design into its more ebullient and exaggerated Baroque mode – the effects and modes of Villa Lante, say, emerging in the later Villa Aldobrandini, and therefore explained perhaps as a transitional mode between early Renaissance garden art and its later, early seventeenth-century manifestations. Might it not be the case that the very ways in which visitors responded to the earlier gardens – one thinks of the evidence provided by Montaigne, Wotton and Guerra – had a palpable effect on how the later ones like Aldobrandini accommodated what had clearly been a significant kind of reception? We might then see later work as providing spatial and formal opportunities for experiences freshly learnt and articulated in earlier gardens.

Another interesting field of enquiry could address English garden design and experience around 1900. This period saw an explosion of garden writings on both design and experience (sometimes blurring them), and it would be possible to demonstrate that despite the prominence given by historians to the stylistic battle between the architectural designers, on the one hand, and those who favoured the 'wild' or naturalistic garden, on the other, it was the effect on each of experience in the other that effected a new and very modern resolution of a long-standing conflict (or dialogue) between both form and content and between form and its reception, what John Sedding would call, in a some-what gnomic shorthand, a 'garden of betweenity'.[22]

VI

An exhibition of the work of the 'land artist' Hamish Fulton at the Sainsbury Centre for Visual Arts at the University of East Anglia in February 2001 was entitled 'An Object Cannot Compete with an Experience'. For any attention to the reception of land-scape architecture, or to what has here been called the afterlife of gardens, that is a potent claim. It argues for the event not the object, for the undervalued role of a 'recipient' in 'completing art as a performance'.[23] So it might help us – in conclusion – to develop the idea of the 'performance' of a landscape site if we take up an analogy with some more obvious performance piece, such as a stage play or a piece of music.

A dramatic script and a musical score are both products of artists with intentions as to the design, shape and effect of their creation; we might even be lucky and have records – film or sound recordings – of original performances directed by the dramatists or composers themselves. More often than not, however, we have no idea how Shakespeare would have staged his plays or Buxtehude played the organ. So, whether or not the music is performed with historical instruments or the play has characters speak in purportedly original speech-patterns, every subsequent performance will deliver a new version of the work (however much we yearn for access to an 'original' experience). Thus it is that we have developed histories of interpretation or performance, where either the individual performances are considered interesting for their own sakes or, more radically, we learn to appreciate a stage play or piece of music as the sum total of a series of interpretations or responses. The cultural accretions that gather around, say, *Hamlet* or Mozart's opera

Don Giovanni effectively augment our understanding of those works as original compositions. Such accretions are not, however, like those that form on shipwrecked objects like anchors or guns, distorting and even disguising their original shape and purpose; rather they enrich imaginatively what is now an *ur-text* with a palimpsest of response. That interpretative vision perhaps lay behind W. H. Auden's claim for the afterlife of W. B. Yeats's poetry, whereby 'the words of a dead man are modified [we might now say "performed"] in the guts of the living'.

That provides one answer to the questions that, on behalf of reception study carried over into landscape architecture, may be asked of literary reception theory – what does it achieve? what is it used for? Clearly the study of reception of a literary text draws out the fullest potential of its meanings – not every reader 'gets it' at once or in one reading any more than does one visitor or one visit to a landscape; secondly, it reveals how different readings are elicited by different cultural conditions. A plausible metaphor for or even model of this palimpsestial reception of a site may be one developed by Ian McHarg for ecological analysis.[24] He proposed the layering of different schemes of knowledge about a site – its hydrology, geology or flora and fauna, its circulation patterns, its residue of inhabitation and so on – as a prelude to grasping fully what any new intervention in that particular site would entail. With the more sophisticated digital techniques of almost half a century later we can well imagine mapping the different responses of a series of visitors to a site over time – tracking the various stimuli, whether built items or natural features, and then the various kinds of reception that each of the stimuli promoted perhaps at different periods. The materials for such a projection would have to be researched and discovered, just as McHarg and his colleagues did with the sites that they explored.

Every visitor brings different resources of 'memory and anticipation'[25] to a place, as witness in recent history the contested appreciations and readings of Maya Lin's Vietnam Memorial in Washington, DC. It is the conspectus of these that constitutes the full meaning of that place. And for sites more extensive spatially than the Vietnam Memorial the fullest appreciation of their wholeness, their *Gestalt*, ultimately resides in the mind and imagination of a given visitor whose experience has been exposed to 'deambulatory space and peripatetic vision',[26] which implies always a transformation of space. And, further, it is so to speak a collection of such *Gestalten* in the figure of an Implied Visitor that fully honours the complexity of a place. Wolfgang Iser was quoted in chapter One as explaining reception as a 'series of changing viewpoints'; this can be operative for landscape architecture in both the time of an individual's movement through a site and the site's transformation as different visitors have moved through it during its lifetime.

Finally, two further aspects of this Implied Visitor deserve comment. The first is simply that to trace the afterlife of a garden will necessarily focus on individual sites; this will emphasize particularity and locality at the expense of generalized notions of design history, which need to be refined considerably if the study of gardens and designed landscapes is to extend its scope and current achievements. To study the mechanisms of response and experience in a specific place will yield more convincing models for contemporary designers than the often tired reiterations of historical stylistic change and its consequences.

Secondly, the present moment of a site, whether at its inception or at some later date, is an infinitesimally small part of its existence. It was Thomas De Quincey who imaged this idea as the Roman *clepysdra* or water clock, where an upper reservoir of water represents the future, from which drops will regularly form and fall, and the lower container is the past that has received, drop by drop, every instant of that present. Landscapes, too, exist with a large hinterland of elements and responses, and they will receive in their future many more responses and maybe even more physical elements that designers or simple inhabitation and usage will add; their present moment by contrast is fleeting and fragile. Accordingly, designers are wise to address the two more substantial 'containers' of past and future experience and to base their design projections on some dialogue between them.

Bernard Lassus' strategy is to invent or discover in his sites a past event – imaginary for his aptly named Jardin de l'Antérieur (see illus. 22), historical for the quarries at Crazannes (see illus. 74), a mixture of the two at Nîmes-Caissargues (see illus. 75) – on which he then projects narratives for subsequent visitors to read as they will; he certainly anticipates responses and moves to direct them. A different procedure is that of the Swiss landscape architect Georges Descombes, who laid out a 'Swiss way' or path around Lake Uri to celebrate the 700th anniversary of the Swiss Confederation.[27] He and his collaborators invoked and emphasized whatever historical traces could be discovered along the route, not in the spirit of archaeology, but for a 'potential future' in which people walking the trail might speculate or find provisional and temporary meanings.

Descombes' process recalls a distant and culturally very different mode of design as narrated in the eighteenth-century Chinese novel, *The Story of the Stone*. In its seventeenth chapter[28] a newly laid-out garden of some scope and complexity is toured by a party of relations and intimate *cognoscenti* who are invited to compete in devising inscriptions and nomenclature for each building and scene. At issue is both the inventiveness of every supplement proposed for the physical structures and the aptness and resonance of its associations; there is the further suggestion that the variety of responses on this occasion may be different when the patron for whom the garden has been made comes to make her own decisions as to how to 'read' and respond to the elaborate scenery put in place for her enjoyment. The difference between the fictional Chinese example and Descombes' project is the latter's much more minimal physical intervention in the site, while preserving the opportunities for just as rich an associative reception.

A final example of the projection upon a future visitation of ideas or associations or narratives taken from the past might be the poetic installation of another Swiss landscape architect, Paolo Bürgi, at the summit of the Cardada funicular above Locarno (illus. 83 and 84). Three main installations – a belvedere breathtakingly cantilevered out above the valley towards Lago Maggiore, a geological observatory higher up the mountain, and a 'Ludic Path' that lies between them – invite visitors to engage in a fuller understanding of the natural world and its processes. On the walk of the belvedere are inscribed symbolically the stages of growth from seed to fruit; the observatory, with its repertoire of different rocks and more inscribed surfaces, recalls with simple eloquence the long ages of geological time; the Ludic Path offers a series of games, all of which demonstrate to those walkers who engage in them some basic laws of physics,

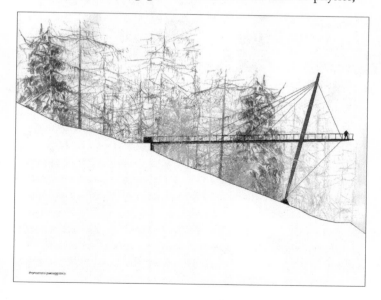

83 Paolo Bürgi, *The Landscape Walk*, a drawing for Cardada, above Locarno.

acoustical or mechanical. The resources for such a landscape of interaction have been drawn by Bürgi from long-established stories; yet what is enthralling about his design is that he has projected how they will be taken up and performed by future visitors (and not incidentally that he will monitor these receptions).

A garden without an afterlife is worth little. In this landscape architecture differs from the art of painting: Velázquez can enjoy an afterlife in Manet, but we can keep the two separate and do allow ourselves an experience of the Spaniard's work independent of the Frenchman's. Visitors to a garden, especially those who bring to their visits imagination, memory and a predisposition to fresh experience, will shift, expand and refocus the site as they find it, and the site will be the larger and more exciting for that reason. It has been observed how odd it is that uniquely in this branch of the design arts we must value 'secondary sources' – whether design documents ('the image, black and white dots on a paper') or visitors' accounts of landscapes – because 'the designer, the architect, the patron, the garden – landscape and plant materials alike – are all gone'. This from an institution that catalogues and identifies the records of American landscape architecture; yet what is also curious in that observation is that the reception of gardens *per se* is marginalized and the 'afterlife of gardens' seems to have no role to play in a historian's establishing of 'aesthetic theories'.[29] The study of how gardens have been experienced will need a determined effort to gather the materials for such an analysis of reception. But that provides the study of gardens with its own extended existence – another afterlife.

References

ONE

A Reception History of Landscape Architecture

1 Of the famous Baroque garden in the Netherlands, Heemstede, its
   leading scholar writes that it was much visited, but few records of visitation survive (Erik de Jong, *Nature and Art: Dutch Garden and Landscape
   Architecture, 1650–1740*, trans. Ann Langenakens, Philadelphia, 2000,
   p. 67). However, it seems to me that the absence of adequate records
   of visitation for many gardens that were well known is due as much to
   our lack of curiosity to search them out or to their being scattered in
   places where garden historians would not customarily think of looking
   or to the fact that we do not interpret other items – engraved views,
   for example – as a record of reception rather than design. If we were
   to feel the need to undertake an alternative, reception history, perhaps
   we might be forced to extend or modify our researches.
2 Recent examples of a designer's or creator's narrative would be
   Douglas Chambers, *Stony Ground: The Making of a Canadian Garden*
   (Toronto, 1996); Lawrence Halprin, *The Sea Ranch . . . Diary of an Idea*
   (Berkeley, CA, 2002).
3 I have relied on the following surveys and discussions of reception
   theory, most of which indicate the *mare maggiore* of further reading:
   Jane P. Tomkins, ed., *Reader-Response Criticism: From Formalism to
   Post-Structuralism* (Baltimore, MD, and London, 1980); R. C. Holub,
   Reception Theory: A Critical Introduction (London and New York, 1984),
   and Elizabeth Freund, *The Return of the Reader: Reader-Response Criticism*

(London, 1987), particularly the sixth chapter.

4 Freund, *Return of the Reader*, p. 150.

5 See W. K. Wimsatt, with Monroe C. Beardsley, *The Verbal Icon: Studies in the Meaning of Poetry* (London, 1954). Their joint essays are also reprinted on many occasions.

6 Freund, *Return of the Reader*, p. 137.

7 See James Elkins, 'On the Conceptual Analysis of Gardens', *Journal of Garden History*, XIII (1993), pp. 189–98, republished in *Our Beautiful, Dry and Distant Texts: Art History as Writing* (University Park, PA, 1997). It would be invidious to give examples of the least strenuous of such effusions, but an example of this mode at its most exciting and useful would be Sir George Sitwell's *On the Making of Gardens* (1909); see the new edition with my forward (Boston, 2003).

8 Freund, *Return of the Reader*, p. 143.

9 I would therefore resist the claim by Denis Cosgrove and Stephen Daniels that 'a landscape park may be . . . no more real . . . than a landscape painting or poem'; for, as they also admit, its palpable existence is as strong as its imaginary. See Cosgrove and Daniels, eds, *The Iconography of Landscape* (Cambridge, 1988), p. 1.

10 Freund, *Return of the Reader*, p. 144.

11 Minna Heimburger-Ravelli, *Disegni di giardini e opera minori di un artista del '700: Francesco Bettini* (Florence, 1981), pp. 47–8 for the full passage describing his experiences at Blenheim.

12 On Versailles see Claire Goldstein, 'Collecting Versailles: Scriptural Economies of the *Cabinet du Roi*', *Studies in the History of Gardens and Designed Landscapes*, XXIII (2003), pp. 258–66. For Stowe and Chiswick, one might consider the commissions to the French artist Jacques Rigaud to record their different sceneries and visitations – see the illustration of these in Peter Willis, *Charles Bridgeman and the English Landscape Garden*, revd edn (Newcastle upon Tyne, 2002), and John Harris, *The Palladian Revival: Lord Burlington, His Villa and Garden at Chiswick* (New Haven, CT, and London, 1994).

13 On both sites there is material that effectively constitutes the basis of a reception history, to which I am indebted here: for Méréville, François d'Ormeson and Pierre Wittner have compiled a record of the site through its many phases – *Aux jardins de Méréville: promenade à la Belle Époque* (Neuilly, 1999); while Vera Schwarcz and Hui Zou have explored

how different responses to Yuanming constitute a whole larger than the sum of its parts – see respectively 'The Garden in Its Time: Visions of Refuge in One Corner of Beijing' and 'The Jing of a Perspective Garden', in *Studies in the History of Gardens and Designed Landscapes*, XXIII (2003), pp. 265–92 and 293–326. See also Young-Tsu Wong, *A Paradise Lost: The Imperial Garden Yuanming Yuan* (Honolulu, 2003).

14 'The Imaginary Garden of Liu Shilong', trans. from the Chinese with a commentary by Stanislaus Fung, *Terra Nova*, II (1997), pp. 15–21.

15 See John Dixon Hunt, *The Picturesque Garden in Europe* (London, 2002), for more detailed explorations both of the terms by which it was described and the responses it elicited.

16 On the imaginative receptions or constructions of Eden, see Charles W. J. Withers, 'Enlightenment and the Paradise Question', in *Geography and the Enlightenment*, ed. David N. Livingstone and Charles W. J. Withers (Chicago, 1999), pp. 67ff., and Georges-Olivier Chateaureynard and Georges Lemoine, *Le Jardin d'Eden* (Paris, 1992); see also for a repertoire of imagery Marie-Therese Gousset, with the collaboration of Nicole Fleurier, *Eden: le jardin médiéval à travers l'enluminure XIIIè–XVIè siècle* (Paris, 2001).

17 James Corner, *Recovering Landscape: Essays in Contemporary Landscape Architecture* (New York, 1999), p. 9.

18 On this theme, see John Dixon Hunt, *Greater Perfections: The Practice of Garden Theory* (London and Philadelphia, 2001), chapters 5 and 6.

19 See Hans-Georg Gadamer, *Truth and Method*, ed. and trans. Garrett Barden and John Cumming (New York, 1975), chapter 2, section b, part ii.

20 C.C.L. Hirschfeld, *Theory of Garden Art*, ed. and trans. Linda B. Parshall (Philadelphia, 2001), p. 6. See also her essay 'Motion and Emotion in C.C.L. Hirschfeld's *Theory of Garden Art*', in *Landscape Design and the Experience of Motion*, ed. Michel Conan (Washington, DC, 2003), pp. 35–52.

21 *The Compleat Gentleman* (1634 edn), pp. 104–6.

22 One of my colleagues at the University of Pennsylvania, James Corner, urges this privileging of 'the imaginary' over 'the built' in 'advancing landscape as an innovative practice': see Corner, *Recovering Landscape*, p. 5, but that imaginary must also involve the plausible reception of designs.

TWO

The Garden as Virtual Reality

1 I was introduced to MYST by a paper read by James Yoch at the Third
International Conference of Word and Image Studies, Dublin, in
September 1996. See also Stephane Natkin, 'Jeux video: le labyrinthe
comme principe d'écriture', in *Labyrinthese du mythe au virtuel*, exh. cat.,
Bagatelle, Paris (2003).

2 Produced in the USA by Corbis (Bellevue, WA, 1996); see the *New York
Times Book Review*, 15 September 1996, p. 23. Both this and the MYST
example (in the previous note) will by now doubtless be technically
outmoded and lost in cyber trash.

3 See *New York Times*, 17 September 1995.

4 I am grateful to Timothy Duffield, a sculptor and landscape architect,
for introducing me to digital projections; and to David Rubin for
examples of work with cybertime.

5 See the special issue on garden archaeology, *Journal of Garden History*,
XVII (1997).

6 Lassus published his proposals first in a privately printed volume, *Le
Jardin des Tuileries* (London, 1991), then in his *The Landscape Approach*
(Philadelphia, 1998), pp. 143–9.

7 Meanwhile, however, see Louise Dampierre, *Digital Gardens: A World in
Mutation*, exh. cat. (Toronto, 1995). See also Mark Slouka, *War of the
Worlds: Cyberspace and the High-Tech Assault on Reality* (New York, 1996),
for a more sceptical view.

8 Eugenio Battisti, '*Natura artifiosa* to *natura artificialis*', in *The Italian
Garden*, ed. David R. Coffin (Washington, DC, 1972), pp. 1–36; here
p. 1 note 3.

9 I would exclude here the garden images by the Canadian photographer
Geoffrey James, taken with a camera that captures precisely these
wide-angle, stereoscopic views: see *The Italian Garden* (New York, 1991)
or *Genius Loci* (Montreal, 1986).

10 For instance, Victor Turner, *The Ritual Process* (Ithaca, NY, 1969), or
Arnold van Gennep, *The Rites of Passage* (Chicago, 1960).

11 Henry Wotton, *Elements of Architecture* (London, 1624), pp. 109–10.

12 See John Dixon Hunt, *Greater Perfections: The Practice of Garden Theory*
(London and Philadelphia, 2001), chapter 3, and Tom Beck, 'Gardens

as a "Third Nature": The Ancient Roots of a Renaissance Idea', *Studies in the History of Gardens and Designed Landscapes*, XXII (2002), pp. 327–34.

13 In a sentence omitted from the passage quoted earlier, Wotton refuses to give any further description of the 'incomparable' garden, because – as he says – 'that were poetical'; by which he might simply have meant that description is the business of poetry and not of an architectural treatise.

14 John Worlidge, *Systema Agriculturae* (London, 1669), folio D1 verso.

15 See variously Marco Berberi, *Bomarzo: un giardino alchemico del cinquecento* (Bologna, 1999); Maurizio Calvesi, *Gli incantesimi di Bomarzo: il sacro bosco tra arte e letteratura* (Milan, 2000); Hella S. Haase, *Les Jardins de Bomarzo* (Amsterdam, 1968; French trans., Paris, 2000); Michiel Koolbergen, *In de ban van Bomarzo* (Amsterdam, 1984).

16 See the first part of John Dixon Hunt, *Garden and Grove: The Italian Renaissance Garden in the English Imagination* (London, 1988).

17 On the Villa d'Este and its iconography, see David R. Coffin, *The Villa d'Este at Tivoli* (Princeton, NJ, 1960), chapter 6, and Claudia Lazzaro, *The Italian Renaissance Garden* (New Haven, CT, 1990), chapter 9; Michel Conan, 'The Conundrum of Le Nôtre's Labyrinthe', in *Garden History: Issues, Approaches, Methods*, ed. John Dixon Hunt (Washington, DC, 1992); on Stowe's Elysian Fields, see John Dixon Hunt, *Gardens and the Picturesque* (Cambridge, MA, 1992), pp. 77–85.

18 William Gilpin, *A Dialogue upon the Gardens at Stow* (1748), ed. John Dixon Hunt, Augustan Reprint Society Publication no. 176 (1976), and Louis XIV, *Manière de montrer les jardins de Versailles* (Paris, 1992).

19 Louis Carrogis, called Carmontelle, *Jardin de Monceau* (Paris, 1779); see the excellent essay on this site by David Hays, "'This is Not a Jardin Anglais: Carmontelle, the Jardin de Monceau, and Irregular Garden Design in Late Eighteenth-century France', in *Villas and Gardens in Early Modern Italy and France*, ed. Mirka Benes and Diane Harris (Cambridge, 2001), pp. 294–326.

20 'Si l'on peut faire d'un Jardin pittoresque une pays d'illusions, pourquoi s'y refuser? On ne s'amuse que d'illusions; si la liberté les guide, que l'Art les dirige, et l'on ne s'éloignera jamais de la nature. La nature est variée suivant les climats; essayons, par des moyens illusoires, de varier aussi les climats, ou plutôt de faire oublier celui où nous sommes; transposons, dans nos Jardins, les changements de scène des opéras;

faisons-y voir, en réalité, ce que les plus habiles Peintres pourraient y
offrir en décoration, tous les temps & tous les lieux. Qu'il soit permis
d'éviter cette froide monotonie, produite par des préceptes prétendus
sévères, qui contraignent l'imagination. Pluisqu'il faut tout créer; usons
de cette liberté pour plaire, pour amuser et pour intéresser. C'était ce
que comptaient trouver, dans le jardin de Monceau, ceux que venaient
le voir; puisqu'ils disaient, quand il y avait peu de choses, j'aimerai
autant me promener dans la compagne. On s'attendait donc à trouver
ce qu'on ne voit pas ordinairement ailleurs' (p. 4).

21 See the short essay, John Dixon Hunt, 'A Dream of Old Europe:
    Crowninshield Garden, Delaware', *Landscape*, September 1988,
    pp. 48–53.

22 I am grateful to the artist for information on these various projects.
    See also John Angeline's discussion of another project by Boyer,
    this time in New York, in the *Journal of Garden History*, XVI (1996),
    pp. 298–309.

23 On Japelli, see Raymond W. Gastil, 'Jappelli's Gardens: "In Dreams
    Begin Responsibilities"', in *The Italian Garden: Art, Design and Culture*
    (Cambridge, 1996), pp. 274–301.

24 See both John Dixon Hunt, 'Les temps de l'histoire et l'invention de
    lieu', in *Les temps du paysage*, ed. Philippe Poullaouec-Gonidec, Sylvain
    Paquette and Gérald Domon (Montreal, 2003), pp. 60–61, and Peter
    Jacobs, 'Après Baudelaire: quoi de neuf?', *Studies in the History of
    Gardens and Designed Landscapes*, XXIII (2003), pp. 328–39.

THREE

Experiencing Gardens and Landscapes in the
Hypnerotomachia Poliphili

1 See his journal *De voyage en Italie par la Suisse et l'allemagne en 1580 et 1581*
   (Paris, 1955). These features are discussed by Lionello Puppi, 'Nature
   and Artifice in the 16th-century Italian Garden', in *The Architecture of
   Western Gardens*, ed. M. Mosser and G. Teyssot (Cambridge, MA, 1991),
   pp. 47–58.

2 See *Libri di immagini, disegni e incisioni di Giovanni Guerra*, exh. cat.
   (Modena, 1978).

3 The standard Italian edition is the two-volume one by G. Pozzi and
   L. Ciapponi (Padua, 1968; 2nd edn, 1980), to the first text volume of
   which I give all references in the text. There is now a full English
   translation (Thames & Hudson, 1999), and a facsimile of the sixteenth-century French one, *Le Songe de Polifile*, ed. Gilles Polizzi (Paris,
   1994). After references to the modern Italian edition (abbreviated as
   HP), I give, where relevant, parallel references to the French version
   (*Songe*) and to the partial English translation of 1592, *The Strife of Love
   in a Dreame*, intro. Lucy Gent (New York, 1973) (cited as *Strife*). On
   the authorship of this book there is much dispute and a considerable
   literature, but this seems irrelevant to my topic here.

4 Robert Harbison, *Eccentric Spaces* (London and New York, 1977),
   pp. 74, 88.

5 For instance, Stefano Borsi, *Polifilo architetto* (Rome, 1995) or the pre-
   ponderance of concerns with the book's architectural effects at the
   University of Pennsylvania symposium, published as a special issue
   of *Word & Image*, XIV/1 and 2 (1998), despite my own concern as
   convenor and editor to pay due attention also to the landscapes.

6 See Anthony Littlewood, 'Romantic Paradises: The Role of the
   Garden in Byzantine Romance', *Byzantine and Modern Greek Studies*,
   V (1979), pp. 95–114. Also Anthony Littlewood, Henry Maguire
   and Joachim Wolschke-Bulmahn, eds, *Byzantine Garden Culture*
   (Washington, DC, 2002).

7 See his 'L'intégration du modèle: le *Poliphile* et le discours du jardin
   dans *La recepte véritable*', in *Bernard Palissy, 1510–1590*, ed. Frank
   Lestringant (Saint-Pierre-du-Mont, 1992), fig. 4; also reproduced in
   the special issue of *Word & Image*, XIV (1998), p.67, fig. 3.

8 That Poliphilo narrates only after the events and landscape he
   experiences should give him the benefit of retrospection, but the
   author makes nothing of that, leaving us, the readers, with the more
   privileged vision or version of these gardens and landscapes.

9 The remark is Harbison's (*Eccentric Spaces*, p. 81). The acrostic authorship of Francesco Colonna is spelt out in the initial letters of the 88
   chapters composing the sentence that reads 'Poliam Frater Franciscus
   Colonna Oeramavit' (Brother Franciscus Colonna greatly loved Polia).

10 Polizzi, too, makes this comparison: *Le Songe de Polifile*, p. 78 and note
   18. Illustrations of surviving examples of Palissy's ceramic flora and

fauna are found in Leonard N. Amico, *Bernard Palissy: In Search of Earthly Paradise* (Paris and New York, 1996).

11 HP, p. 21, *Strife*, p. 27.

12 HP, p. 48, *Strife*, p. 56.

13 HP, p. 5, *Strife*, p. 11.

14 HP, p. 25, *Strife*, p. 14.

15 'tanto optimamente imitavano la veritate della natura', HP, p. 25, *Strife*, p. 31.

16 HP, p. 26, *Strife*, p. 32.

17 HP, p. 53, *Strife*, p. 63, *Songe*, p. 65. The etymological link to the elder Pliny's *Natural History*, XXXV, 101, is noted in the commentary to the Italian edition of the HP (II, p. 87, being note to 1, p. 53).

18 HP, p. 116, *Strife*, p. 142.

19 To get some sense of the effect probably intended, compare with the plastic flowers that are regularly changed in the modernist flower beds of Emma Tennant, *The Last of the Country House Murders* (London, 1974).

20 A reminiscence of this watery labyrinth is enacted in Robert Irwin's garden at the new Getty Center in Los Angeles.

21 HP, p. 119, *Strife*, p. 146.

22 HP, p. 119, *Strife*, p. 146.

23 HP, p. 133, *Strife*, p. 162.

24 HP, p. 35, *Strife*, p. 44.

25 'la bella et amoena patria, et gli feraci agri et fertili campi'; HP, p. 59, *Strife*, p. 70.

26 Too numerous and lengthy to quote, but see *Strife*, pp. 71–2, 74, 79 and 84.

27 See John Dixon Hunt, *Greater Perfections: The Practice of Garden Theory* (London and Philadelphia, 2001), chapter 3.

28 HP, p. 74, *Strife*, pp. 89–90.

29 Respectively HP, pp. 80–81, pp. 109ff.; *Strife*, pp. 97–8 and 133ff.

30 HP, p. 110, *Strife*, p. 133, *Songe*, p. 115.

31 HP, p. 123, *Strife*, p. 152.

32 HP, p. 188.

33 HP, p. 286, *Songe*, p. 275.

34 See her essay 'Untangling the Knot: Garden Design in Francesco Colonna's *Hypnerotomachia Polifili*', *Word & Image*, XIV (1998),

pp. 82–108.
35　HP, pp. 286ff.
36　HP, p. 286.
37　*Strife*, p. 146.

FOUR

Triggers and Prompts in Landscape Architecture Visitation

1　See John Dixon Hunt, *The Picturesque Garden in Europe* (London, 2002), for more detailed analyses of these strategies.
2　This is what I have previously put forward as an analysis of Stowe's Elysian Fields: see above, chapter Two, note 17.
3　William Gilpin, *A Dialogue upon the Gardens at Stow* (1748), ed. John Dixon Hunt, Augustan Reprint Society Publication no. 176 (1976), pp. 19–20.
4　See Joseph Disponzio, who notes that analogies with the theatre were expected, in his introduction to Watelet's *Essay on Gardens: A Chapter in the French Picturesque*, ed. and trans. Samuel Danon, Penn Studies in Landscape Architecture (Philadelphia, 2003), p. 11 (and see generally in index under 'theater').
5　See the section on pattern books and their use in Hunt, *Picturesque Garden*, pp. 130–33.
6　Joseph Spence, *Polymetis* (London, 1747), pp. 2–3.
7　See the following chapter for some further comparisons between Whately's and Heely's attention to modes of reception in designed landscapes.
8　See, for example, Rosalind Krauss's comment that 'The visual arts have always battled the onslaught of a verbal production – from *ekphrasis* to allegory; from *ut pictura poesis* to iconography – that modernist art managed, briefly, to shun but never totally to silence', *October*, LXXVII (1996), p. 83.
9　See the compelling discussions of this in Indra Kagis McEwen, *Vitruvius: Writing the Body of Architecture* (Cambridge, MA, 2002).
10　In *P.N. Review*, XLII (1982).
11　*The Order of Things* (London, 1970), p. 38.
12　All quotations from Delille's poem noted in the text are from the

edition of 1782.

13 See Giulia Pacini, 'Signs and Sites of Friendship in Delille's *Les Jardins*', *Studies in the History of Gardens and Designed Landscapes*, XXIII (2003). I am indebted to her essay for these perspectives on Delille's poem.

14 Disponzio, in his introduction to Watelet's *Essay on Gardens*, pp. 67–72.

15 As indeed was claimed especially of William Gilpin, the popularizer of the picturesque in England; see W. D. Templeman, *The Life and Works of William Gilpin* (Urbana, IL, 1939), p. 228.

16 McEwen, *Vitruvius*, p. 17, as for the following remark; all other references are included in the text.

17 See Bernard D. Frischer and Iain Gordon Brown, eds, *Allan Ramsay and the Search for Horace's Villa* (London, 2001). More generally, Pierre Grimal, *Les Jardins romains* (Paris, 1969).

18 The following address the issue of meaning in landscape architecture: Robert Riley, 'From Sacred Grove to Disney World: The Search for Garden Meaning', *Landscape Journal*, VII (1983), pp. 136–47; Laurie Olin, 'Form, Meaning and Expression in Landscape Architecture', *Landscape Journal*, VII (1983), pp. 149–68; Marc Treib, 'Must Landscapes Mean? Approaches to Significance in Recent Landscape Architecture', *Landscape Journal*, XIV (1995), pp. 47–62; for a philosopher's viewpoint, see Stephanie Ross, *What Gardens Mean* (Chicago, 1998).

19 Richard Guy Wilson, 'High Noon on the Mall: Modernism versus Traditionalism, 1900–1970', in *The Mall in Washington, 1791–1852*, ed. Richard Longstreth (Washington, DC, 1991).

20 John Barrell has examined this breakdown persuasively in his study *The Political Theory of Painting from Reynolds to Hazlitt* (New Haven, CT, and London, 1976).

21 Stephen Bann, in fact, has described Finlay's concern as 'the simple but fundamental question: how do we confer meanings upon the world', a concern, though, that addresses reception as much as conferral (Alec Finlay, ed., *Wood Notes Wild*, Edinburgh, 1995, p. 65).

22 This could mean, for instance, using only native specimens when replanting an Olmsted park, despite the fact either that Olmsted himself chose to use exotics more than 100 years ago, which is itself an interesting 'meaning' invested in the original design. That those 'exotics' have by now become natives along the way – green card holders, so to speak – is an extra meaning for an Olmsted design that we surely must

also accept.

23 For Simon, see *Studies in the History of Gardens and Designed Landscapes*, XXIII (2003), pp. 224–6; for Kienast, see his *Lob der Sinnlichkeit* (Zurich, 1999), p. 42.

24 This painting is reproduced in John Dixon Hunt, '"Come into the Garden, Maud": Garden Art as a Privileged Mode of Commemoration and Identity', *Places of Commemoration: Search for Identity and Landscape Design*, ed. Joachim Wolschke-Bulmahn (Washington, DC, 2001), fig. 3.

25 See McEwen, *Vitruvius*, p. 34.

26 Quoted in McEwen, *Vitruvius*, p. 61.

27 I have discussed this briefly in *Greater Perfections: The Practice of Garden Theory* (London and Philadelphia, 2001), but revisit the site here because it contributes so crucially to my argument.

28 Stephan Bann has drawn attention to Finlay's fascination with the gnomic Delphic inscription of an $\sum$ (epsilon) about which Plutarch meditates: see *Wood Notes Wild*, p. 78.

29 On Rousseau, see Hunt, *Greater Perfections*, pp. 176–7; for Proust, see Michel Conan, '*Puer aeternus* in the Garden', *Studies in the History of Gardens and Designed Landscapes*, XXIX (1999), pp. 86–101.

30 *Wood Notes Wild*, pp. 220–33.

31 Yves Abrioux, *Ian Hamilton Finlay: A Visual Primer*, 2nd edn (London, 1992).

32 Quoted in *Wood Notes Wild*, p. 59.

33 Ian Hamilton Finlay and Kathleen Lindsley, folding card (Wild Hawthorn Press, n.d.), showing scene across the lake at Stourhead, Wiltshire, with the aphoristic definition printed inside.

FIVE
Verbal versus Visual Responses in Garden Visitation

1 *A Particular Account of the Emperor of China's Gardens near Pekin*, trans. Joseph Spence (London, 1752), p. 46.

2 R. Hatfield, 'Some Unknown Descriptions of the Medici Palace in 1459', *Art Bulletin*, LII (1970), p. 253. This source also contains the original Italian and some visual materials on the garden.

3 Henry Wotton, *Elements of Architecture* (1624), pp. 109–10, text

modernized; perhaps referring to either the Medici villa at Pratolino or the Villa d'Este at Tivoli.

4 The most accessible version is reprinted in *The Genius of the Place*, pp. 96–9.

5 Roy Strong, *The Renaissance Garden in England* (London, 1979), p. 145.

6 Leon Battista Alberti, *On the Art of Building in Ten Books*, trans. Joseph Rykwert, Neil Leach and Robert Tavernor (Cambridge, MA, 1991), p. 317 (Book 9, section 10).

7 See below in chapter Seven.

8 I rely here primarily on his collection, *Descriptions of Lord Cobham's Gardens at Stowe, 1700–1750* (Buckinghamshire Record Society, 1990), to which further references are made in the text. But see also both his edition of George Bickham's *The Beauties of Stow* (1750), Augustan Reprint Society (Los Angeles, 1977) and my own edition of William Gilpin, *A Dialogue upon the Gardens at Stow* (1748), Augustan Reprint Society Publication No. 176 (1976). A collection of Stowe descriptions and guides was also issued by Garland reprints, *The Gardens at Stowe*, ed. John Dixon Hunt (New York, 1982).

9 George Clarke, 'The Gardens at Stowe', *Apollo*, XCVII (June 1973), p. 558. In the introduction to the collection of *Descriptions* he gives an abbreviated version of these design developments (pp. 8–12).

10 The unsigned plan was published with engravings signed by 'Rigaud and Baron' and has itself never been attributed: it is, however, in the style of John Rocque who was making a name for himself by producing garden plans (Wanstead 1735, Chiswick 1736 [see illus. 61], Claremont 1738); it would have been appropriate for Sarah Bridgeman to turn to Roque to produce a plan to accompany her husband's posthumous publication of views of the Stowe gardens.

11 See George Clarke, 'Where Did All the Trees Come From? An Analysis of Bridgeman's planting at Stowe', *Journal of Garden History*, V (1985), pp. 72–83.

12 I use here the first English translation by Samuel Danon, *Essay on Gardens: A Chapter in the French Picturesque*, with an introduction by Joseph Disponzio, Penn Studies in Landscape Architecture (Philadelphia, 2003); in-text page references are to this translation. This edition also includes what graphic representations of the site survive and the site plan from about 1780 preserved in the French

National Archives, some of which are reproduced here.

13 These are the words of one of Girardin's section headings: see *An Essay on Landscape* (New York, 1982), p. 134.

14 See above, p. 102.

15 *Coup d'oeil at Beloil and a Great Number of European Gardens*, trans. and ed. Basil Guy (Berkeley, CA, 1991), pp. 188–9.

16 See above, chapter Four, note 15.

17 The reference is to the discussion of different arts in Lessing's *Laokoön* (1766): see the modern translation by Ellen Frothingham (New York, 1957).

18 F. de Latapie, trans., *L'Art de former les jardins modernes; ou, l'art des jardins anglois* (Paris, 1771), pp. lii–liii (my translation of Latapie's French). Latapie did in fact include a map of Stowe in his version of Whately's book.

19 See Ian J. Lochhead, *The Spectator and the Landscape in the Art Criticism of Diderot and his Contemporaries* (Ann Arbor, MI, 1981). For the early literature on the *paragone*, see the French anthology *Le Paragone: le parallele des arts*, ed. Lauriane Fallay D'Este (Paris, 1992).

20 Girardin, *Essay on Landscape*, p. 50.

21 This point is made by Norman Bryson, *Art and Text in Ancient Greek Culture*, ed. Simon Goldhill and Robin Osborne (Cambridge, 1994), p. 266.

22 Bryson, *Art and Text*, p. 10.

23 Lessing, *Laokoön*, trans. Ellen Frothingham (New York, 1957), primarily pp. 91 and 109 for paintings' distinctive qualities, and pp. 91, 100 and 139 for those of poetry.

24 The reference is to his discussion on pp. 150–51, for a commentary on which see John Dixon Hunt, 'Emblem and Expression in the 18th-century Landscape Garden', in his *Gardens and the Picturesque* (Cambridge, MA, 1992), pp. 75ff.

25 Galen A. Johnson, in *Encyclopedia of Aesthetics*, ed. Michael Kelly, 4 vols (New York and Oxford, 1998), vol. II, p. 205. See *The Merleau-Ponty Aesthetics Reader*, ed. Galen A. Johnson (Evanston, IL, 1993) for the detailed analyses of Cézanne on which this summary is based.

26 See also Katja Grillner, *Ramble, Linger and Gaze: Dialogues from the Landscape Garden* (Stockholm, 2000) for other contrasts and comparisons between the two writers. It is worth noting that Heely's original edition

(Birmingham, 1775) was entitled a *Description . . .* , and it was only in the London edition two years later that he called them *Letters . . .* All references here are to this later edition.

27 'A Revisal . . . ' occupies pp. 185 ff. in this second edition; quotations in my text are from pp. 154, 189 and 192 respectively.

28 Perhaps Mason was simply envious of the success of Whately's book on a subject that Mason had promoted 27 years earlier in a volume that seems to have passed unnoticed.

29 William Watts, *The Seats of the Nobility and Gentry in a Collection of the Most Interesting and Picturesque Views* (1779); William Angus, *The Seats of the Nobility and Gentry in Great Britain and Wales* (1787); William Birch, *Les Délices de la Grande Bretagne* (1791).

SIX
The Role of Movement in Garden Reception

1 Thomas Whately, *Observations on Modern Gardening*, p. 50, commenting on Kent's hillside design for Claremont; Claude-Henri Watelet, *Essay on Gardens: A Chapter in the French Picturesque*, ed. and trans. Samuel Danon, Penn Studies in Landscape Architecture (Philadelphia, 2003), p. 50.

2 It is also worth noting, given my reliance on Watelet throughout these essays, that he also wrote an essay on movement for his *Dictionnaire des arts de peinture, sculpture et graveur* (Paris, 1792), vol. III.

3 The attention of Dadaists, Surrealists and Situationists to walking the city is explored by Francesco Careri, *Walkscapes: El andar como practica estetica / Walking as An Aesthetic Practice* (Barcelona, 2002), with a detailed list of further readings (I am grateful to Philippe Coignet for directing me to this book). Yet the modern interest may begin earlier: see John Gay, *Trivia; or, The Art of Walking the Streets* (London, 1717), and Karl Gottlob Schelle, *Die Spatziergange oder die Kunst spatzieren zu gehen* (1788), available in a French translation, *L'Art de se promener* (Paris, 1996). A cultural history of walking in the broad Romantic period is offered by Gudrun M. König, *Eine Kulturegeschichte des Spaziergangs: Spuren einer burgerlichen Prattik, 1780–1850* (Vienna, 1996). There is also the important work of Michel de Cerceau, *Practice of Everyday Life*, trans. S. Randell (Berkeley, CA, 1984), which treats of our perambulatory experience in

the city.

4 Careri, *Walkscapes*, p. 11.

5 *Histoire de la disposition et des formes différents que les chrétiens ont données a leurs temples . . .* (Paris, 1764), pp. 56–7. I take this example from Yves Alain Bois, 'A Picturesque Stroll around *Clara-Clara*', *October*, XXIX (1984), pp. 41–3, who in his turns borrows it from Peter Collins, *Changing Ideals in Modern Architecture* (Montreal, 1965), p. 26.

6 Henry Wotton, *Elements of Architecture* (1624), p. 4.

7 Byzantine Constantinople provides an important example of an existing urban site used for processional purposes: see John F. Baldwin, SJ, *The Urban Character of Christian Worship: The Origins, Development and Meaning of Stational Liturgy* (Rome, 1987).

8 I use a modern edition with an introduction by Allen Weiss (Paris, 1999), p. 49.

9 *Manière de montrer les jardins de Versailles par Louis XIV*, with introduction by Simone Hoog (Paris, 1992), p. 32. There are many similar injunctions in these guided tours.

10 The first of these festivities was recorded by Israel Silvestre in eight engravings, the second in a series by Jean Le Pautre, and the third by a set from Le Pautre with François Chauveau. Verbal accounts of these events were also published: see A. Marie, *Naissance de Versailles: le château – les jardins*, 2 vols (Paris, 1968), vol. I, pp. 44–50, vol. II, pp. 327–35, and vol. II, pp. 336–42, respectively.

11 Louis Carrogis, called Carmontelle, *Jardin de Monceau* (Paris, 1779), p. 4.

12 The National Trust now has its own guide; under the auspices of Stowe School was produced one by Laurenece Whistler, Michael Gibbon and George Clarke, *Stowe: A Guide to the Gardens*, 3rd edn (Buckingham, 1974).

13 David R. Coffin has drawn upon such commentaries on major sites in his *The Villa in the Life of Renaissance Rome* (Princeton, 1979), pp. 327ff. for the Villa d'Este and pp. 347ff. for the Villa Lante at Bagnaia. The direction and preparation of visitors at such sites by available materials needs more exploration beyond the concerns of iconographical analysis.

14 *The Letters of the Young Pliny*, trans Betty Radice (Harmondsworth, 1963), pp. 75–9 and 139–44.

15 See Guillaume de Loris and Jean de Meun, *Le Roman de la rose*, trans.

and ed. Frances Horgan (New York, 1994). The French poem was originally translated into English by Geoffrey Chaucer. For many illustrations of the lover's ritual procession through the different spaces, see John Harvey, *Mediaeval Gardens* (London, 1981) and Marie-Therese Gousset, *Eden: le jardin medieval . . .* (Paris, 2001), among other sources.

16 Careri, *Walkscapes*, p. 22.

17 Stephen Switzer, *Ichnographia Rustica* (London, 1718), vol. II, p. 197.

18 See chapter Five, pp. 122–3.

19 Joseph Heely, *Letters on the Beauties of Hagley, Envill and the Leasowes* (1777), vol. I, pp. 67–8.

20 See for example the discussion by Stanislaus Fung, 'Movement and Stillness in Ming Writings on Gardens', in *Landscape Design and the Experience of Motion*, ed. Michel Conan (Washington, DC, 2003).

21 Scudéry , *Promenade de Versailles*, p. 20.

22 Scudéry, *Promenade de Versailles*, pp. 45 and 53.

23 See his *Description sommaire du Château de Versailles* (Paris, 1674): I owe this reference to Claire Goldstein.

24 For a full survey of the views of Chiswick, see John Harris, *The Palladian Revival: Lord Burlington, his Villa and Garden at Chiswick* (New Haven, CT, and London, 1994).

25 Hal Moggridge, surveying the gardens in the 1980s, calculated that there were 1,064 ways to stroll without ever repeating one's route: see 'Notes on Kent's Garden at Rousham', *Journal of Garden History*, VI (1986), p. 191.

26 Mavis Batey, 'The Way to View Rousham by Kent's Gardener', *Garden History*, XI (1983), pp. 125–2.

27 G. R. and C.C. Collins, commenting on Sitte's *Der StadteBau nach seinen kunstlerischen Grundsatzen* (1889), in their *Camillo Sitte and the Birth of Modern City Planning* (New York, 1986), pp. 120–21.

28 See F. Hamilton Hazlehurst, *Gardens of Illusion: The Genius of André le Nostre* (Nashville, TN, 1980), and, on Dampierre, his essay in *Tradition and Innovation in French Garden Art* (Philadelphia, 2002), pp. 44–67.

SEVEN

Moving Along in the Automobile

1 Although the French landscape architect Bernard Lassus has rightly
 argued that air travel has a crucial impact on landscape reception
 (it turns, for instance, oceans into ponds), I will not deal here with
 various attempts from Schipol to Dulles airports to design landscapes
 to be experienced by sky travellers. And in this segment I will also
 focus primarily on road travel, with which Lassus himself has been
 preoccupied recently.
2 *New York Times*, 22 July 2003.
3 A small chronological sampling of works consulted include W.
 Brewster Snow, ed., *The Highway and the Landscape* (New Brunswick, NJ,
 1959), Sylvia Crowe, *The Landscape of Roads* (London, 1960), Donald
 Appleyard, Kevin Lynch and John R. Myer, *The View from the Road*
 (Cambridge, MA, 1964), and Lawrence Halprin, *Freeways* (New York,
 1966).
4 Respectively, Myer, *View from the Road*, p. 4, and Halprin, *Freeways*, p.29.
5 See Anette Freytag, 'When the Railway Conquered the Garden: Velocity
 in Parisian and Viennese Parks', in *Landscape Design and the Experience of
 Motion*, ed. Michel Conan (Washington, DC, 2003), pp. 215–42. See also
 Wolfgang Schivelbusch, *The Railway Journey: The Industrialization of Time
 And Space in the 19th Century* (Leamington Spa, Hamburg and New York,
 1986).
6 Quoted by Freytag, 'When the Railway Conquered the Garden',
 p. 229, note 21.
7 Freytag, 'When the Railway Conquered the Garden', pp. 238–42. See
 also Melissa Maldonado, 'The Jardin Atlantique', *Studies in the History of
 Gardens & Designed Landscapes*, XX (2000), pp. 297–312, and some
 imagery of it in a catalogue of contemporary French landscape architecture, *Studies in the History of Gardens & Designed Landscapes*, XXIII/2
 (2003), pp. 192–3. For a further example of how railway experience
 may be extended into or connected with landscapes at given destinations, see the project at Cardada, above Lago Maggiore, by the Swiss
 landscape architect Paolo Burgi (below, pp. 221–2).
8 See J. B. Jackson, *A Sense of Place, a Sense of Time* (New Haven, CT, and
 London, 1994), pp. 191 and 6. On Jackson's contribution to the study

of roads, see Timothy Davis, 'Looking Down the Road: J. B. Jackson and the American Highway Landscape', in *Everyday America: Cultural landscape Studies after J. B. Jackson*, ed. Chris Wilson and Paul Groth (Berkeley, CA, 2003), pp. 62–80.

9 This is a theme that concerned J. B. Jackson and is addressed by Timothy Davis in 'Looking Down the Road'.

10 This is an important chapter in a study of landscape reception that I shall not take up in detail here. Timothy Davis has written well and extensively of the parkway movements and its aspirations: see, in particular, his 'Rock Creek and Potomac Parkway, Washington, DC: The Evolution of a Contested Urban Landscape', being a special issue of *Studies in the History of Gardens & Designed Landscapes*, XIX/2 (1999), and his '"A Pleasant Illusion of Unspoiled Countryside": The American Parkway and the Problematics of an Institutionalized Vernacular', *Constructing Image, Identity and Place*, ed. Alison K. Hoagland and Kenneth A Breisch, Perspectives in Vernacular Architecture, IX (Knoxville, TN, 2003), pp. 228–46.

11 Quoted by Michel Conan in his introduction to *Landscape Design and the Experience of Motion* (Washington, DC, 2003), p. 1.

12 *The Landscape Approach*, Penn Studies in Landscape Architecture (Philadelphia, 1998), p. 82, my italics.

13 These are now well known and discussed: the best analysis is that by Michel Conan, 'The Crazannes Quarries of Bernard Lassus', *Studies in the History of Gardens & Designed Landscapes*, XXIII (2003), pp. 347–66.

14 See Lassus' own presentation in *The Landscape Approach*, pp. 164–7, and my own analysis, not to be repeated here, in *Greater Perfections: The Practice of Garden Theory* (London and Philadelphia, 2001). Both texts illustrate elements of the site.

EIGHT
The Afterlife of Gardens and the Implied Visitor

1 From the translation *Essay on Gardens*, the first in English, by Samuel Danon with an introduction by Joseph Disponzio, Penn Studies in Landscape Architecture (Philadelphia, 2003), p. 40.

2 C.C.L. Hirschfeld, *Theory of Garden Art*, ed. and trans. Linda B. Parshall

(Philadelphia, 2001), p. 205; Parshall quotes the same passage in her essay in the Dumbarton Oaks volume, *Landscape Design and the Experience of Motion*, ed. Michel Conan (Washington, DC, 2003), p. 430 (hereafter cited as *Experience of Motion*).

3 Stanisluas Fung seems to be making the same point when he finds a 'blurring of the distinction between primary and secondary sources' in writing on Chinese gardens. See *Experience of Motion*, p. 246.

4 See my discussion of Pope's famous advice in *Greater Perfections: The Practice of Garden Theory* (London and Philadelphia, 2001), p. 9.

5 This distinction is that of Michel Conan, 'Landscape Metaphors and Metamorphosis of Time', *Experience of Motion*, p. 299.

6 Conan, 'Landscape Metaphors', p. 315, note 31.

7 This would also be an instance of an inscription moving its readers in a garden from what Michael Charlesworth has called a 'mythic' to a 'real' space, giving actuality to a previously metaphoric possibility: see his 'Movement, Intersubjectivity and Merchantile Morality at Stourhead', in *Experience of Motion*, p. 285.

8 In this connection, see Michael Leslie, 'History and Historiography in the English Landscape Garden', *Perspectives on Garden Histories*, ed. Michel Conan (Washington, DC, 1999), pp. 91–106.

9 For the Villa d'Este and Villa Lante see references above in chapter Six, note 13; for a contemporary example take Laurie Olin, 'What I Do When I Can Do It: Representation in Recent Work', *Studies in the History of Gardens and Design Landscapes*, XIX (1999), pp. 102–21.

10 A selection of these are, in chronological order: Kenneth Woodbridge, 'Henry Hoare's Paradise', *Art Bulletin*, XLVIII (1965), pp. 83–116, and his *The Stourhead Landscape*, revd edn (London, 1982); Ronald Paulson, *Emblem and Expression: Meaning in English Art of the Eighteenth Century* (Cambridge, MA, 1972), chapter 2; Max F. Schulz, 'The Circuit Walk of the Eighteenth-century Landscape Garden and the Pilgrim's Circuitous Progress', *Eighteenth-Century Studies*, XV (1981), pp. 1–25; James Turner, 'The Structure of Henry Hoare's Stourhead', *Art Bulletin*, LXI (1979), pp. 68–77; Malcolm Kelsall, 'The Iconography of Stourhead', *Journal of the Warburg and Courtauld Institutes*, XLVI (1983), pp. 133–43.

11 Charlesworth, 'Movement, Intersubjectivity, and Merchantile Morality at Stourhead' in *Experience of Motion*, pp. 263–86.

12 Kelsall, 'Iconography of Stourhead', p. 137.

13 See the new edition (Boston, 2003), respectively pp. 15 and 16–17, among other examples that could be offered.

14 I am indebted to my colleague Anita Berrizbeitia for making me aware of this: see her *Roberto Burle Marx in Caracas: Parque del Este, 1956–1961*, Penn Studies in Landscape Architecture (Philadelphia, 2004), especially chapter Three.

15 An example recently to hand is the discussion by Patricia Johnson in *Experience of Motion*, 'Beyond Choreography: Shifting Experience in Uncivilized Gardens', pp. 75–102, where she explains how she expects visitors to behave in her sites, whether in part conducting them around, relying on narratives known to be familiar to visitors or otherwise inventing ways in which to make people behave in certain ways.

16 *The RSVP Cycles: Creative Processes in the Human Environment* (New York, 1969), p. 2. A detailed analysis of Halprin's book in the light of a reception approach to landscape architecture needs to be undertaken.

17 *Experience in Motion*, pp. 25–31.

18 *Experience in Motion*, p. 3.

19 *Experience in Motion*, p. 308 note.

20 I have argued elsewhere for the (perhaps neglected) usefulness of anthropology as a resource for landscape architecture: see 'Taking Place: Some Preoccupations and Politics of Landscape Study', in *Deterritorialisations . . . : Revisioning Landscapes and Politics* (Edinburgh, 2003), pp. 124–31.

21 Stanislaus Fung suggests a Chinese example, *Experience of Motion*, p. 252; see also his quotation of 'the scene winds in accord with the path', p. 260.

22 On this see Anne Helmreich, *The English Garden and National Identity: The Competing Styles of Garden Design, 1870–1914* (Cambridge, 2002); for Sedding, his *Garden Craft Old and New* (London, 1891), chapter 9.

23 Michael Holly, *Past Looking, Historical Imagination and the Rhetoric of the Image* (Ithaca, NY, 1996), p. 196.

24 As exemplified throughout in Ian McHarg, *Design with Nature* (1969; New York, 1992).

25 Yve-Alain Bois, 'A Picturesque Stroll around *Clara-Clara*', October, XXIX (1984), p. 53, quoting Richard Serra.

26 Bois, 'A Picturesque Stroll', p. 34. See also Francesco Careri, *Walkscapes: El andar como practica estetica / Walking as An Aesthetic Practice* (Barcelona,

2002), p. 50.

27 *Voie Suisse: l'itinéraire genvois: de Morschacha a Bunnen* (Geneva, 1991). Here again we encounter a project in which the designer clearly provides for the reception of his work, yet almost inevitably cannot illustrate its afterlife.

28 I have used the translation by David Hawkes (Bloomington, IN, 1979), pp. 324–47.

29 I take this interesting observation from a *Newsletter* from Wave Hill (XIII/2, Winter 2002) which identifies it as a 'curious phenomenon'.

Photographic Acknowledgements

The author and publishers wish to express their thanks to the below sources of illustrative material and/or permission to reproduce it. In some cases locations of items are also given. All photographs not otherwise acknowledged are by the author or from the author's collection.

Galeazzo Alessi, *Libro dei misteri: Progetto del Sacro Monte di Varallo in Valsesia* (1565–69), ed. Anna Maria Brizio and Stefania Perrone (Bologna, 1974): 56; Archives Départementales des Yvelines et de l'Ancien Département de Seine-et-Oise: 3; Archives Nationales, Paris: 53; photo courtesy of Gilbert Boyer: 21; Bibliothèque Nationale de France, Paris: 54; British Museum, London: 45 (Department of Prints and Drawings, 1962-7-14-50), 59 (MS Add.177), 66; photos courtesy of Paolo Burgi: 82, 83; Trustees of the Chatsworth Settlement: 34, 67; Dumbarton Oaks Collection: 52; Dumbarton Oaks Photo Archive: 58; Graphische Sammlung Albertina, Vienna: 24; Groeningemuseum, Bruges: 77; Gugong Museum, Beijing: 4; Hannema de Stuers Fundatie, Heino, Netherlands: 76; photos courtesy of Bernard Lassus: 71, 72, 73, 74, 75; photo Pierce Lewis: 70; redrawn from *Maniere de montrer les jardins de Versailles*, with introduction and commentary by Simone Hogg (Paris, 1992): 57; Mauritshuis, The Hague (photo A. Dingjan): 8; Musées des Beaux-Arts, Valence (photo Ph. Petiot): 55; Musée Carnavalet, Paris: 16; Musée du Château de Versailles: 64, 78; Musée Départemental Albert Kahn, Boulogne (photo Stephane Passet/© Musée Départemental Albert Kahn): 5; photo courtesy of Ellen Neises: 49; photos Laurie Olin: 15, courtesy of Laurie Olin: 46, 47; diagram redrawn from Gilles Polizzi's doctoral dissertation, 'Emblématique et géometrie l'espace et le recit dans le Songe de Poliphile' (Université de Provence, 1987), with permission of the author: 25; Royal Academy of Fine Arts, Stockholm: 62; Patricia Rubenstein: photos, 7, 18; redrawn diagram: 25; digital imagery by David A. Rubin and Kristina Hill: 9; photos Nancy Patterson Sevcenko: 23, 79; Soon-hui Long, redrawn map: 57; *The 13th Annual Report of the Board of Commissioners of the [New York] Central Park for the Year 1869*: 19; Topographical Museum, Florence: 13; photo courtesy of Marc Treib: 68; University of Pennsylvania Architectural Archives: 48; photo courtesy of the University of Pennsylvania Libraries: 56; by kind permission of Victoria Munroe Fine Art, Boston: 14.

Index